Easy And Relax
Coloring Pages 2

I0475174

Easy Coloring Pages for All Ages

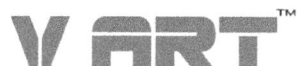

5 Great Ways to Use To Use This Awesome Book

This book is great for fun, meditation, and also for color therapy.

1. You can't do it wrong- You can only do it right!

That is great, isn't it? The designs you will find in this book are made so that you can color them, you can go about this however you like it, you can color inside the lines, or outside the lines, you can also do both, whatever gives you pleasure. You have the choice of choosing whichever pattern or color that you like.

I will also like to inform you that you can use this book for meditation. Here's how:

a. you can select any mandala that calls or attracts you.

b. make your choice of colors, those colors should be those that resonates well with the pattern you have chosen.

c. with joy, begin to color the paper, just flow with it and fill the spaces on each page with color, lines, dots and shapes. You can even use words!

d. Flow with the process! Don't get disconnected.

2. Masculine style mandala coloring

This is an active search for the point of wholeness, of nothingness. Immerse yourself into those patterns, let the noise that's all around you and creating that turmoil fade away, focus on each of the stroke you are making, you will be released as soon as you complete coloring and you will feel refreshed, I guarantee you that.

3. Feminine style mandala coloring

There is an abundance of joy in the world, you've got to find it. This style is a celebration of the abundance of joy. Fill your vision with color. Take pleasure in the caress of your pen. Your fulfillment will be in the process.

4. Make it about someone else

This is very interesting, remember that life is not all about yourself. you can also make this journey about someone else, it will benefit you a great deal. For example: you can choose an important figure to you- like your mother, or father.

Go about coloring it mindfully, as you reflect on every characteristic of such relationship. You will find forgiveness, compassion and understanding. You may even discover a way to celebrate such important relationship. Now, can you just imagine what a blessing that would be? It would be just great.

5. Color therapy

This is also of great advantage for those who need 'color therapy' this book is a very useful tool for color therapy. If a specific chakra requires energy, you have the liberty to select its' color and fill the entire mandala with shades and values of that color.

Now, remember to keep the mandala at a place where it would be very much visible to you, this will help you to focus more on the energies you want to nurture.

Most importantly, mandalas are a wonderful way to enjoy color and quiet doodling for pleasure.

Here is a warning for you: Beware, they are addictive!

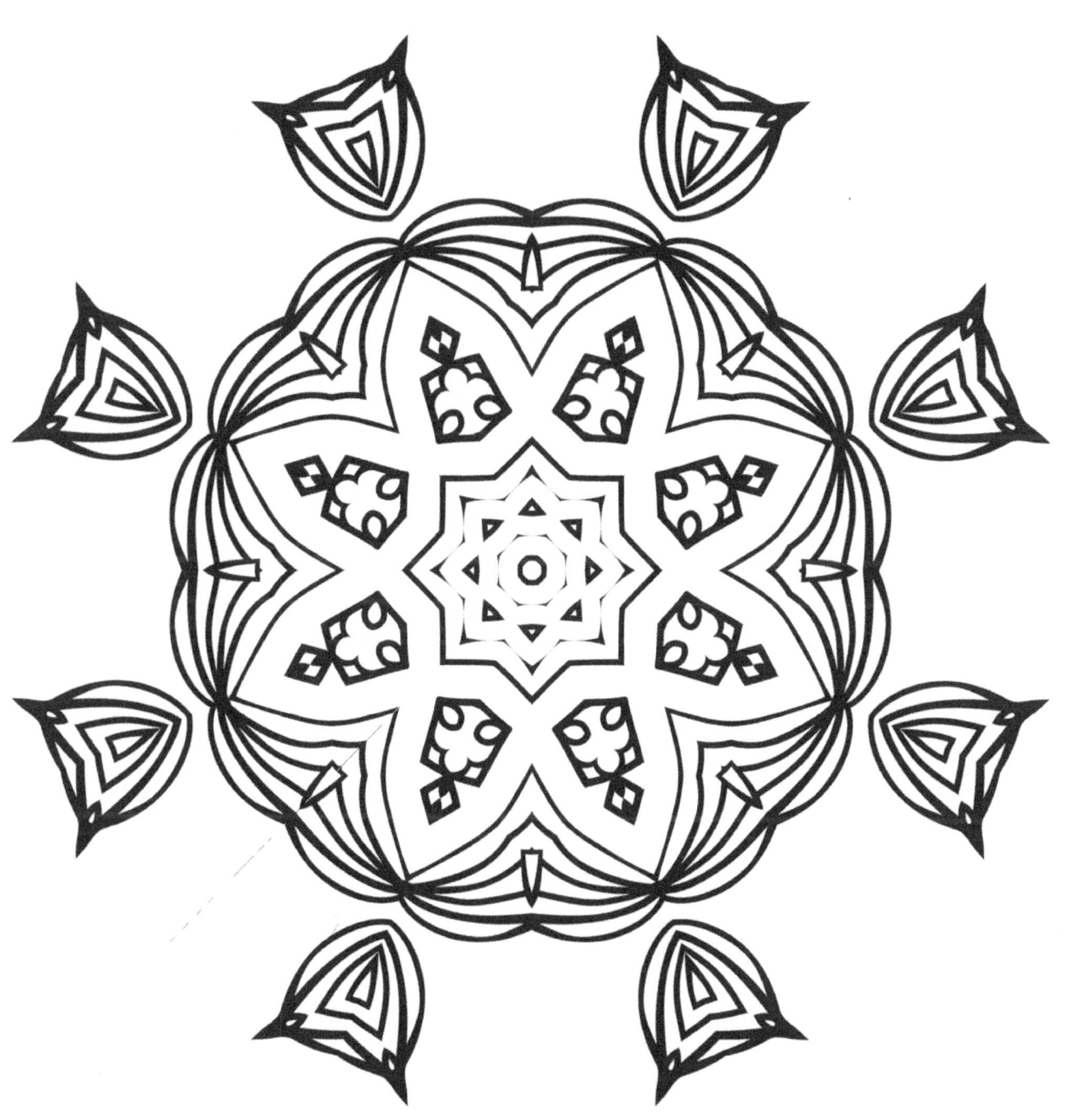

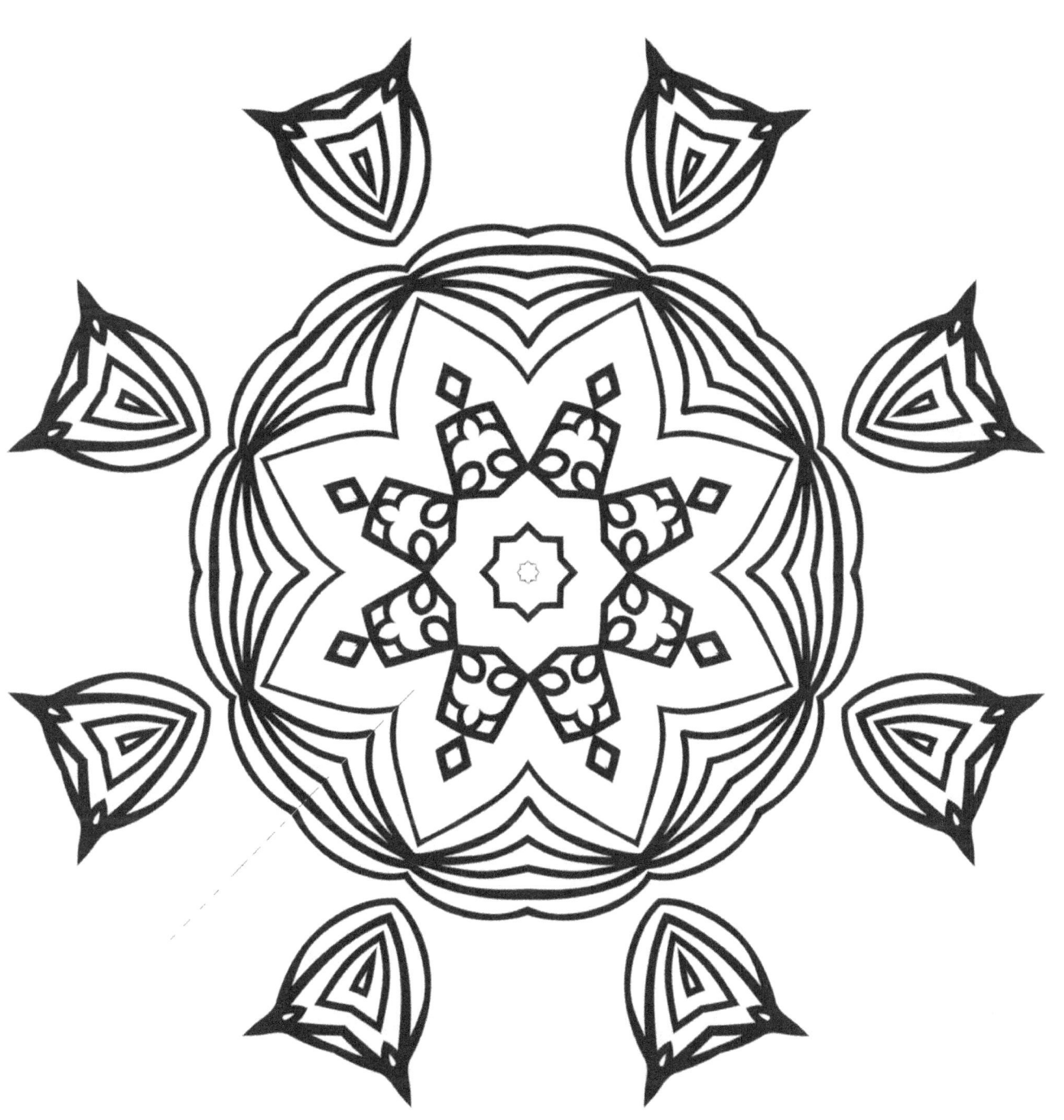

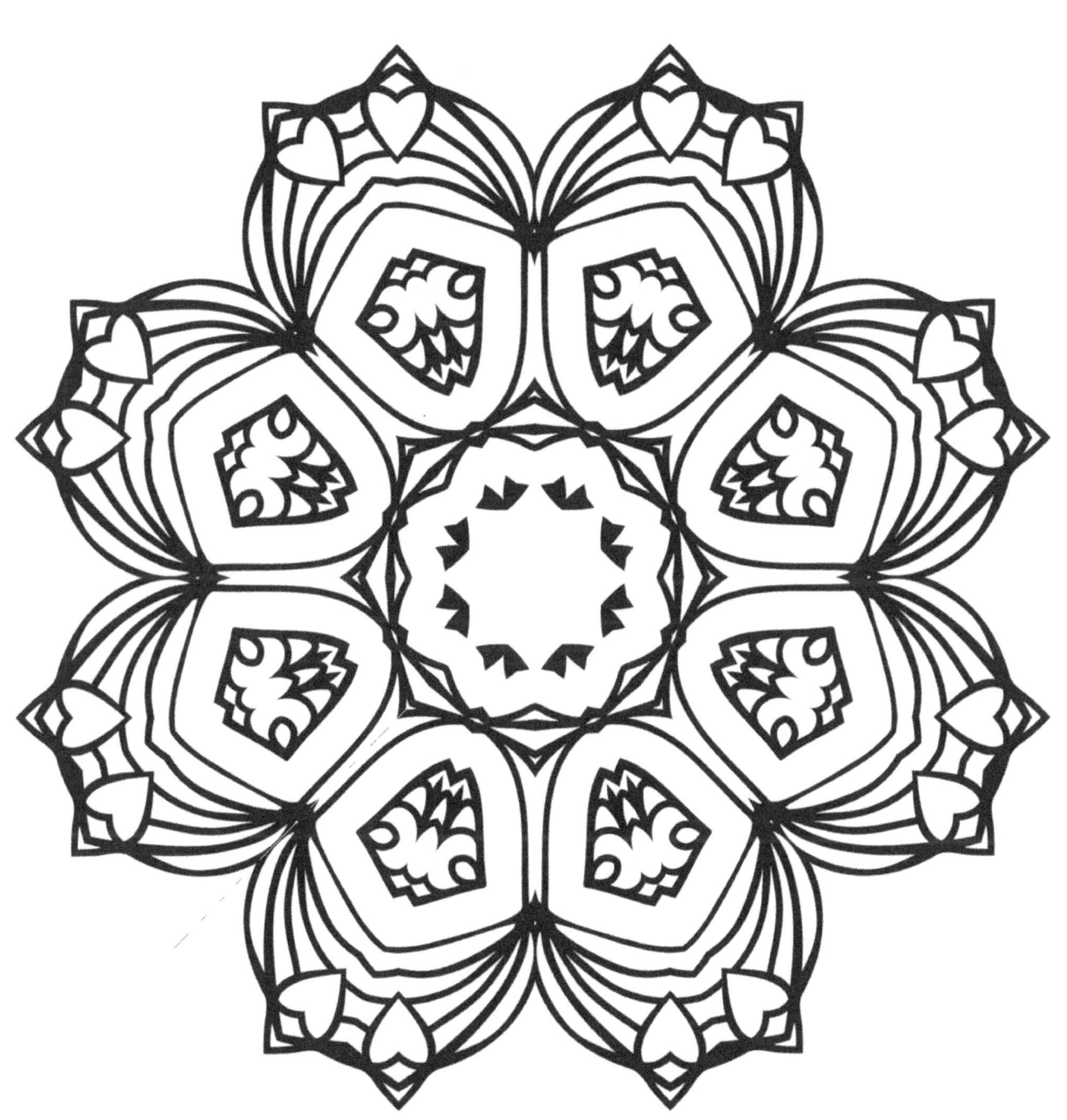

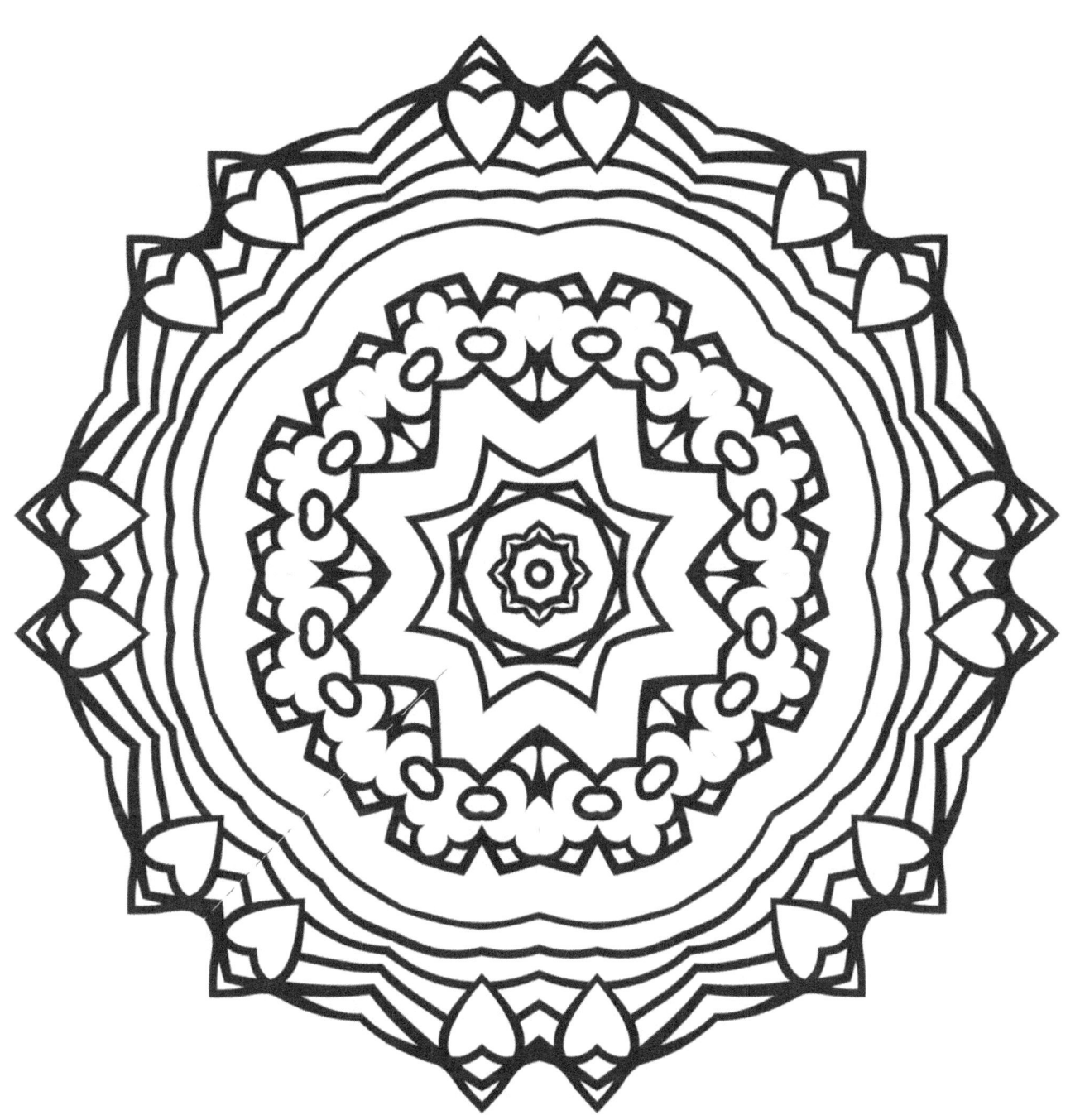

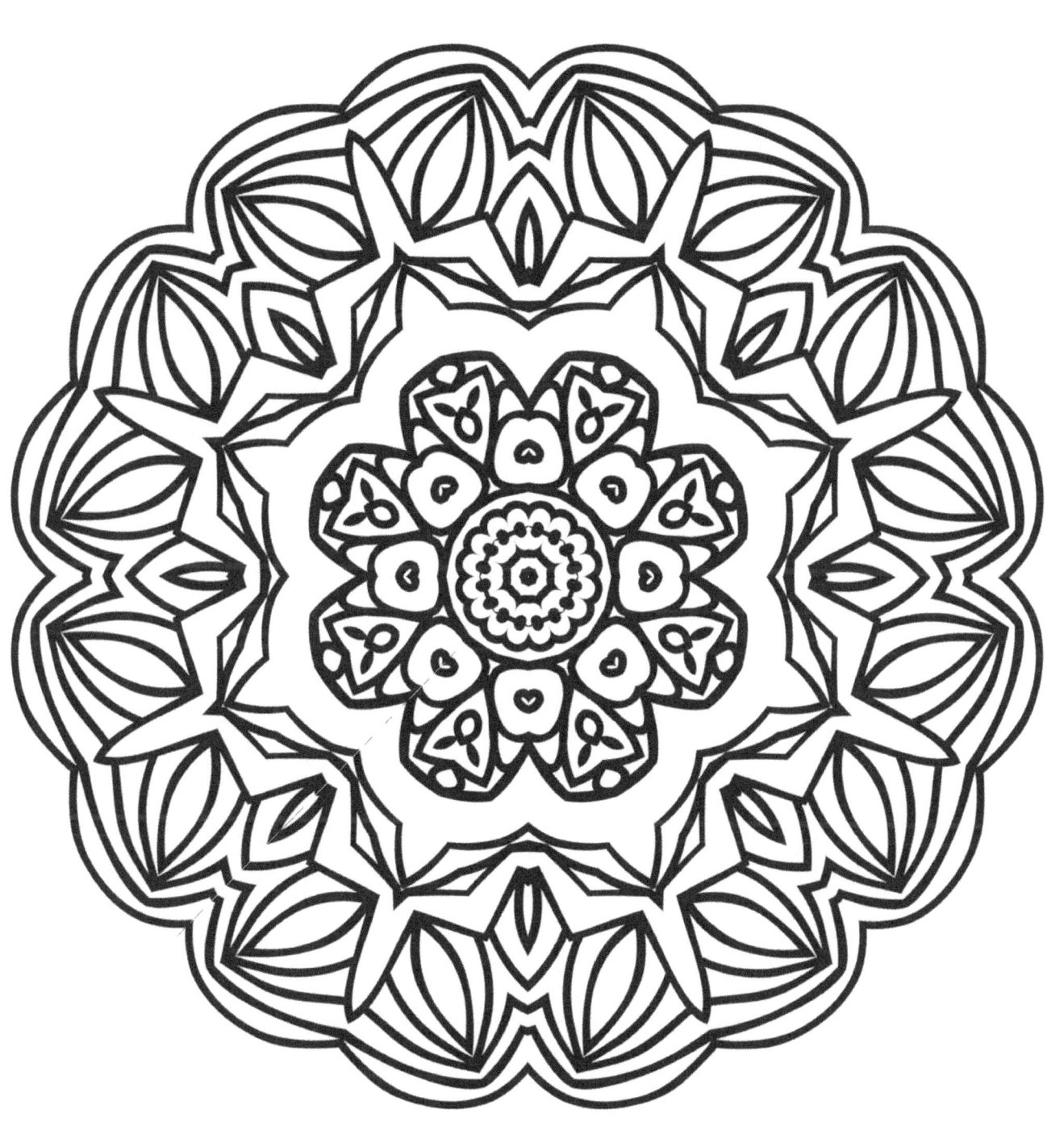

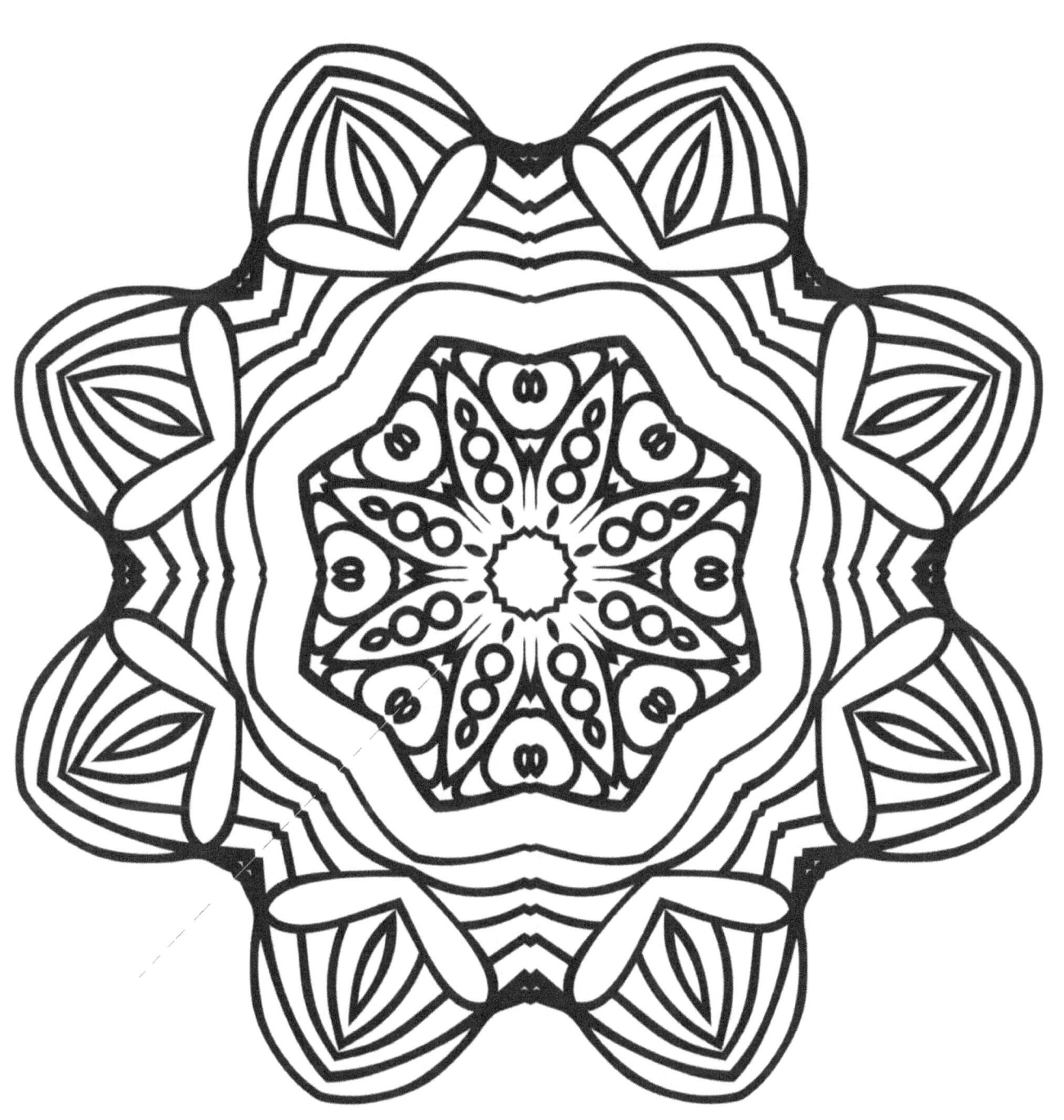

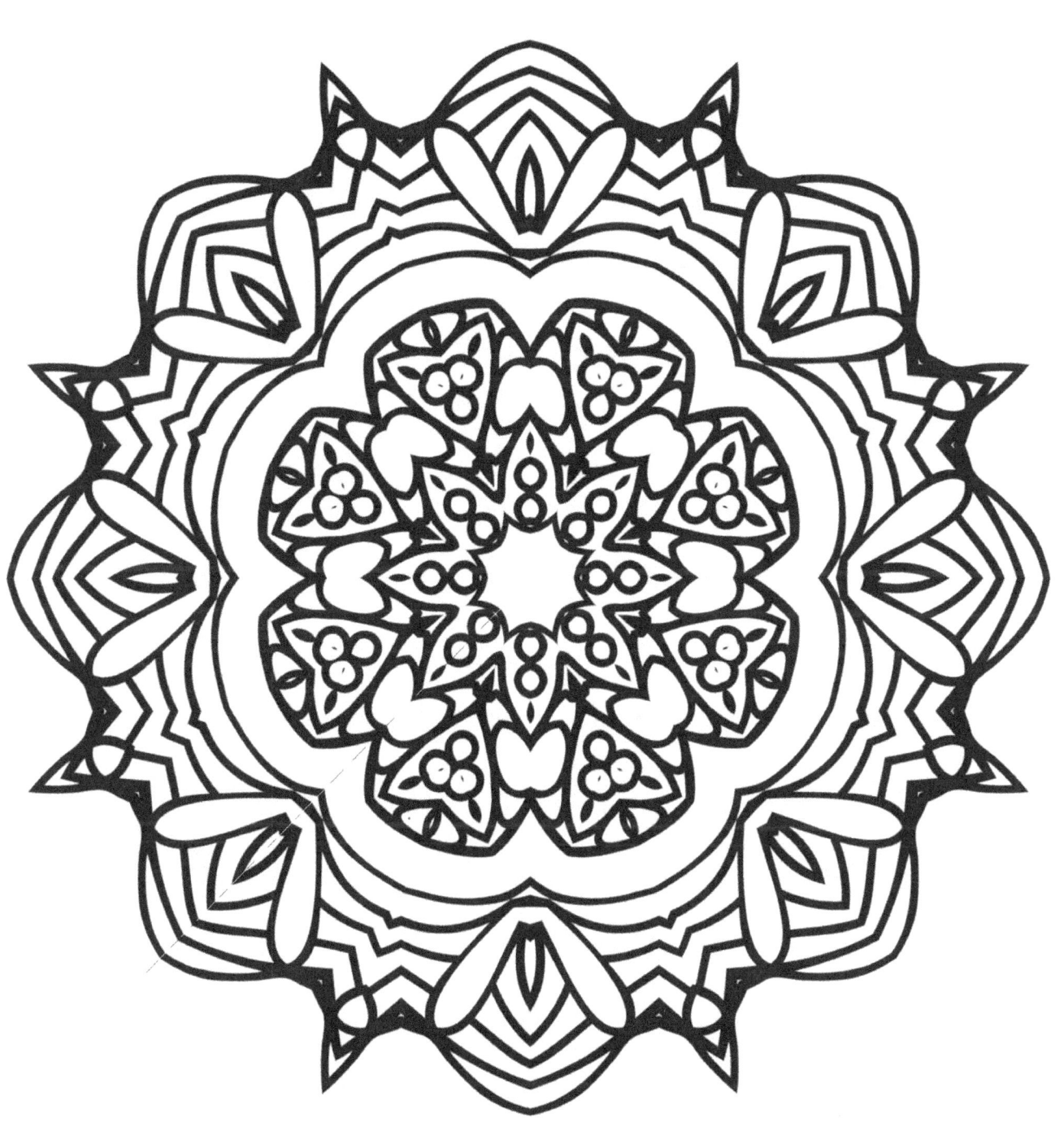

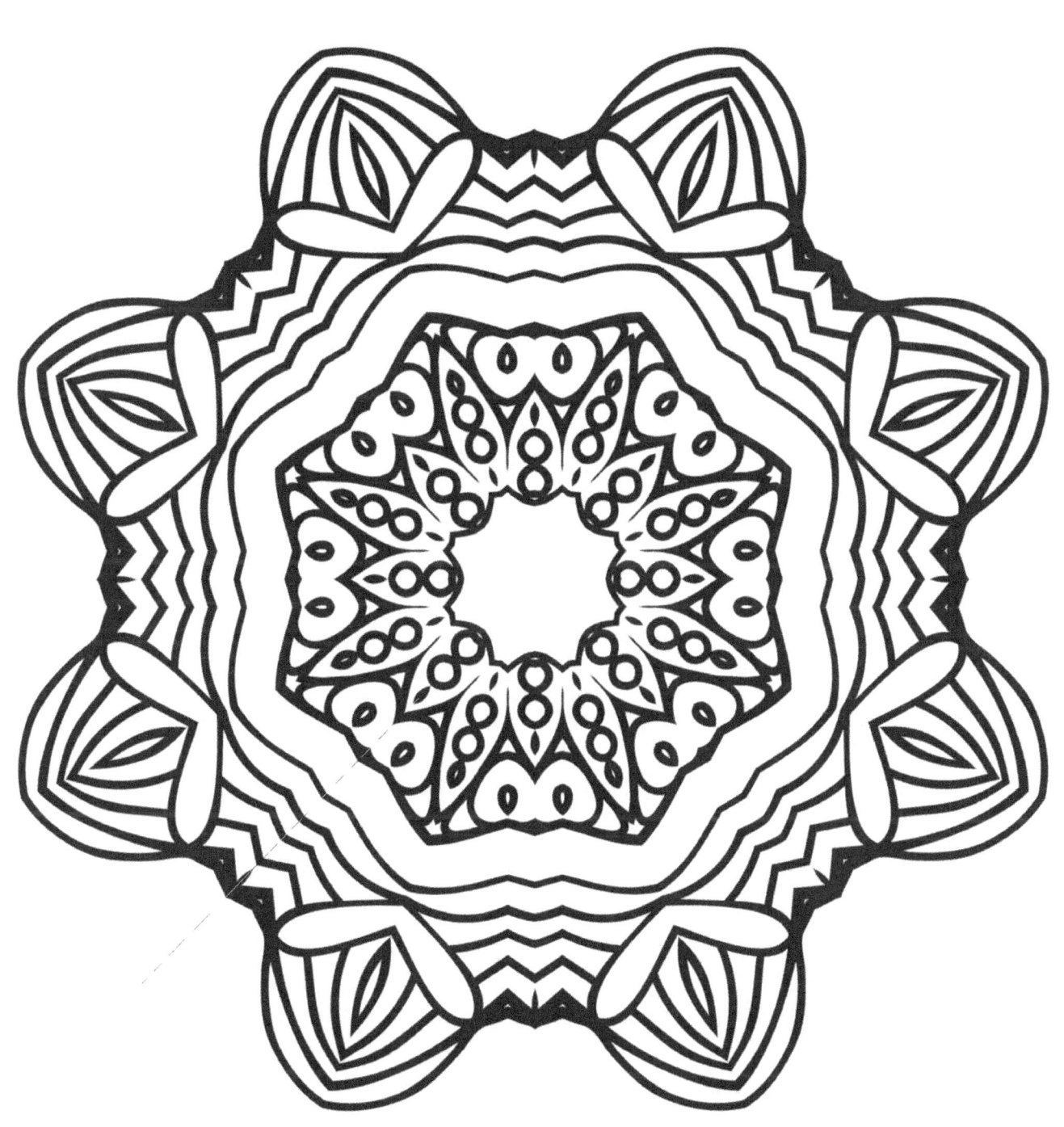

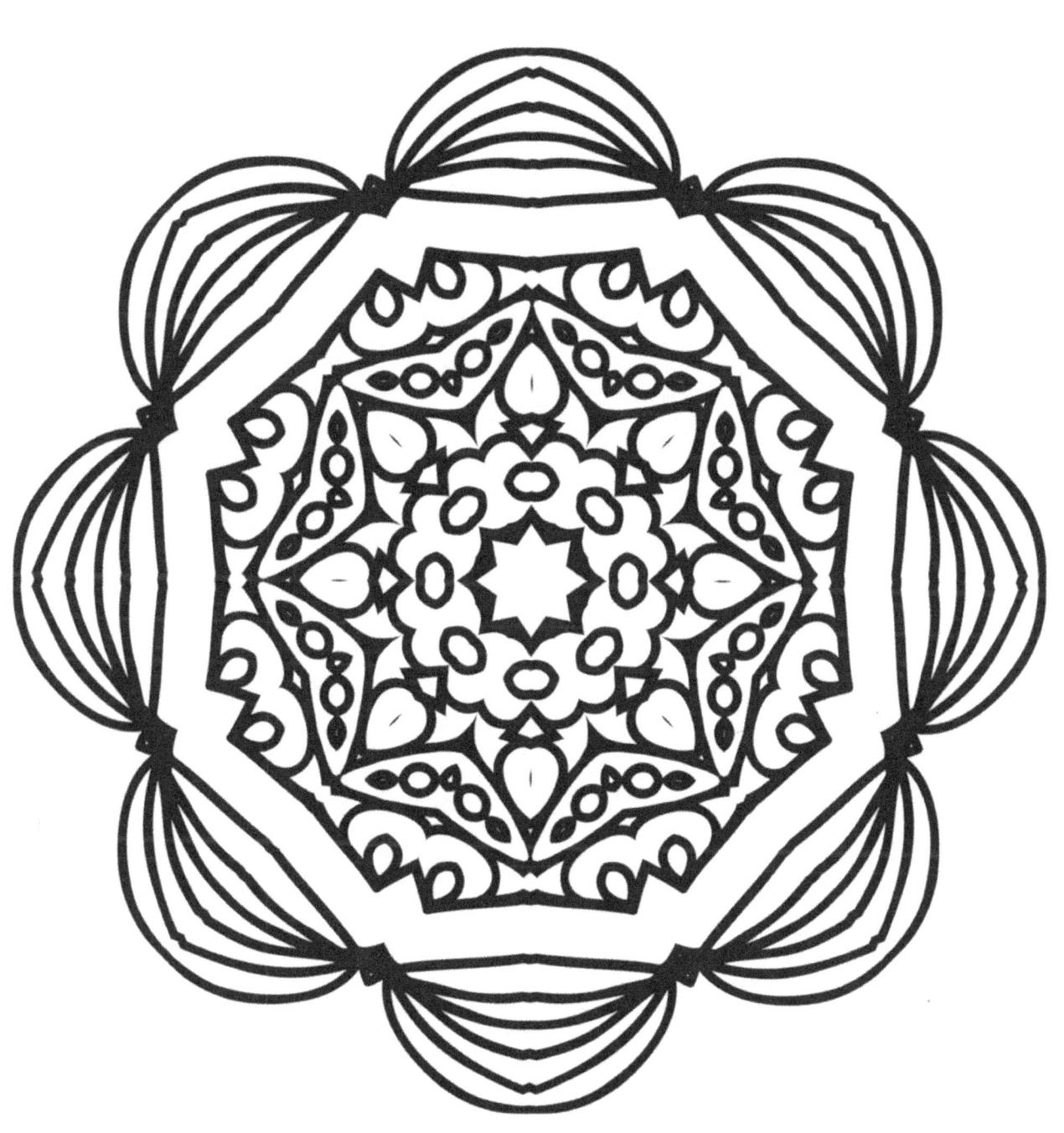

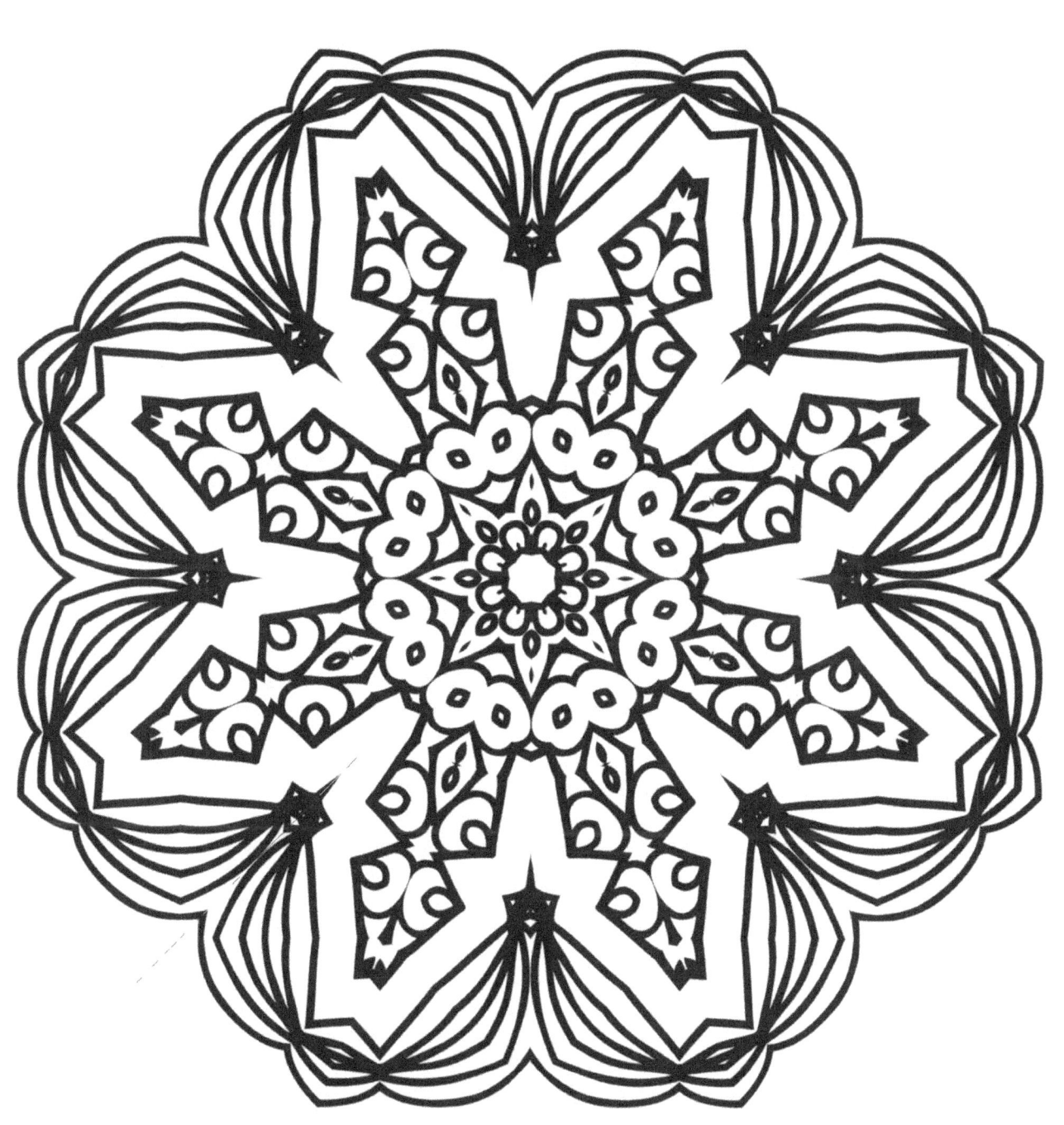

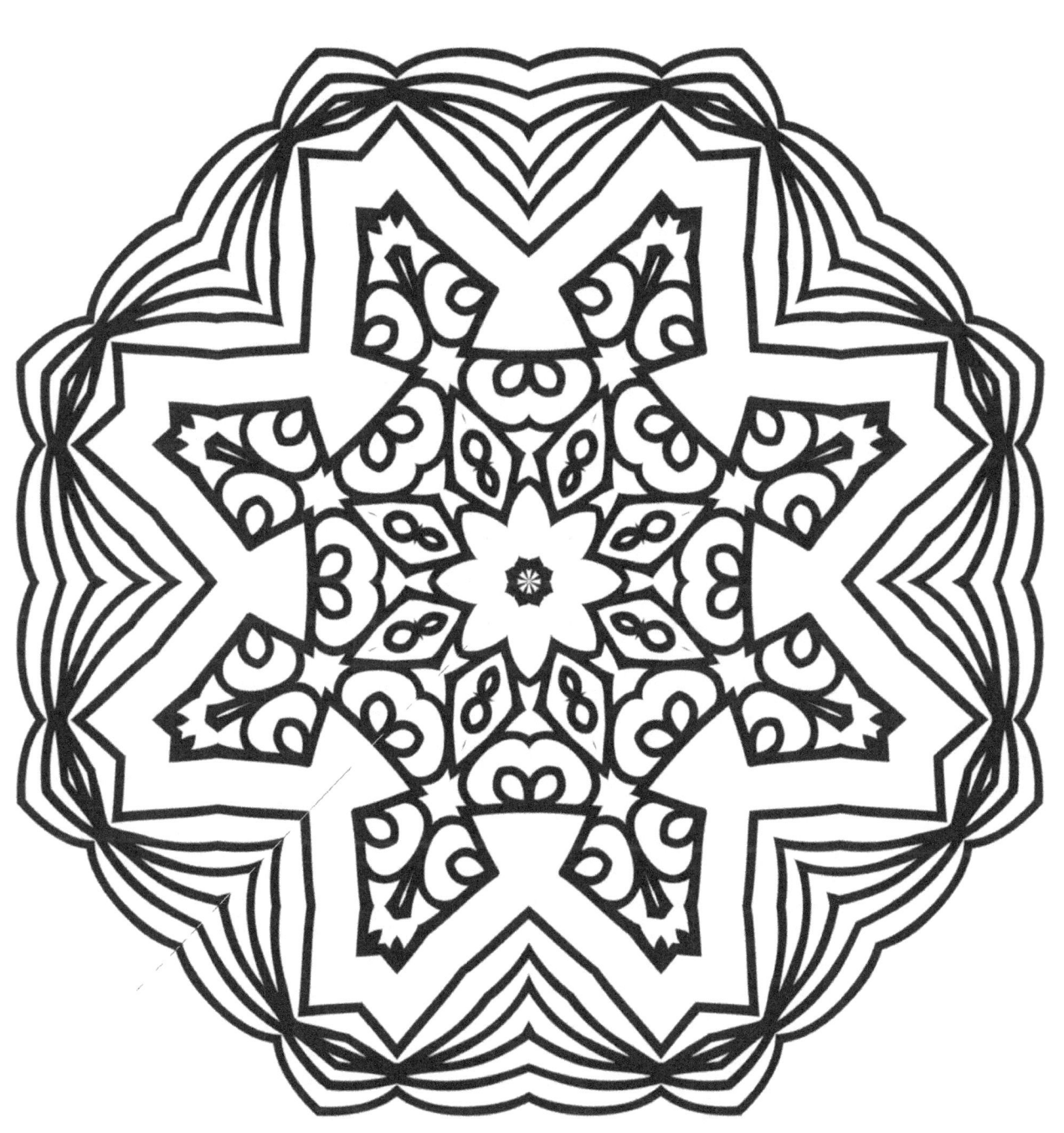

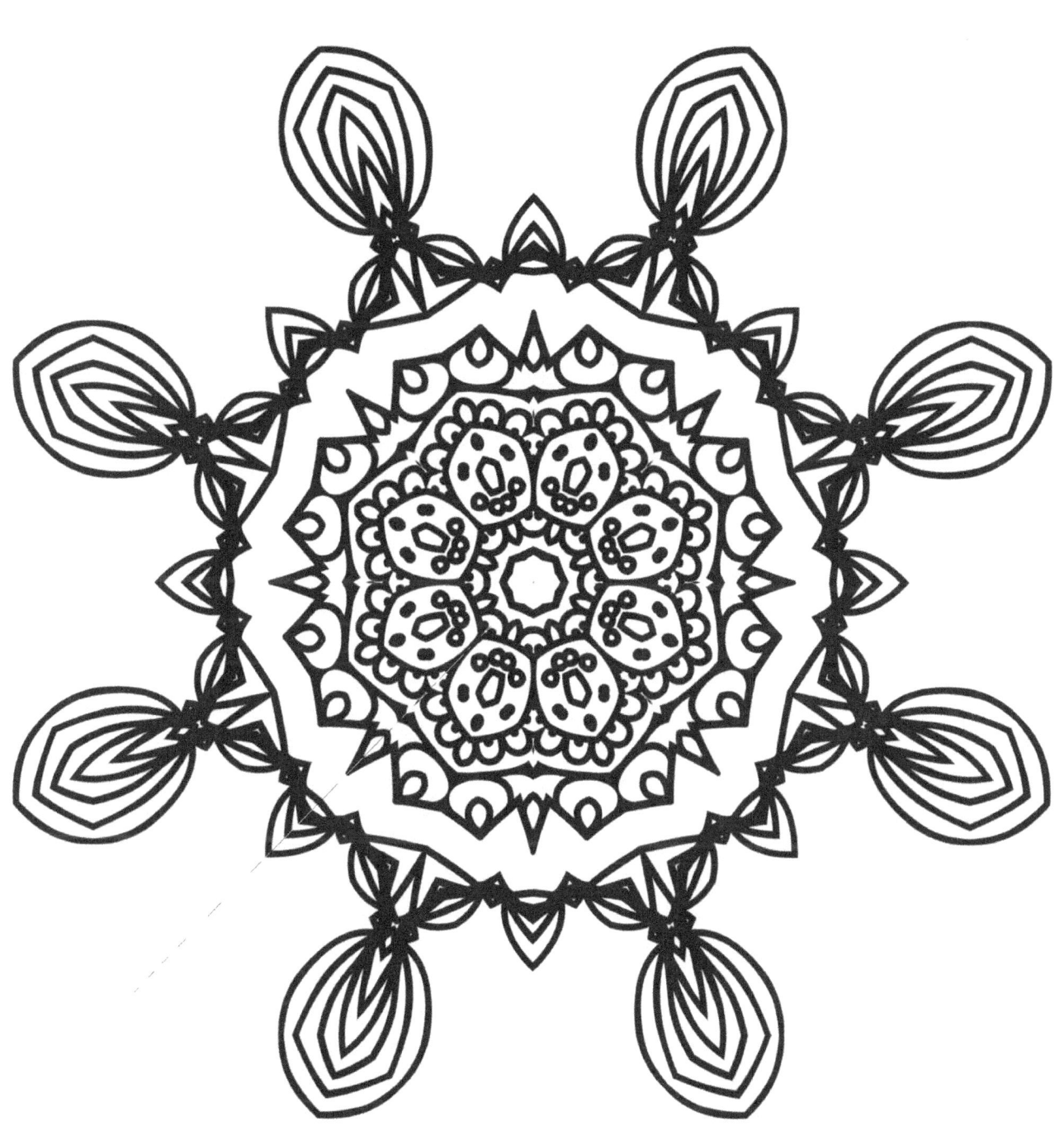

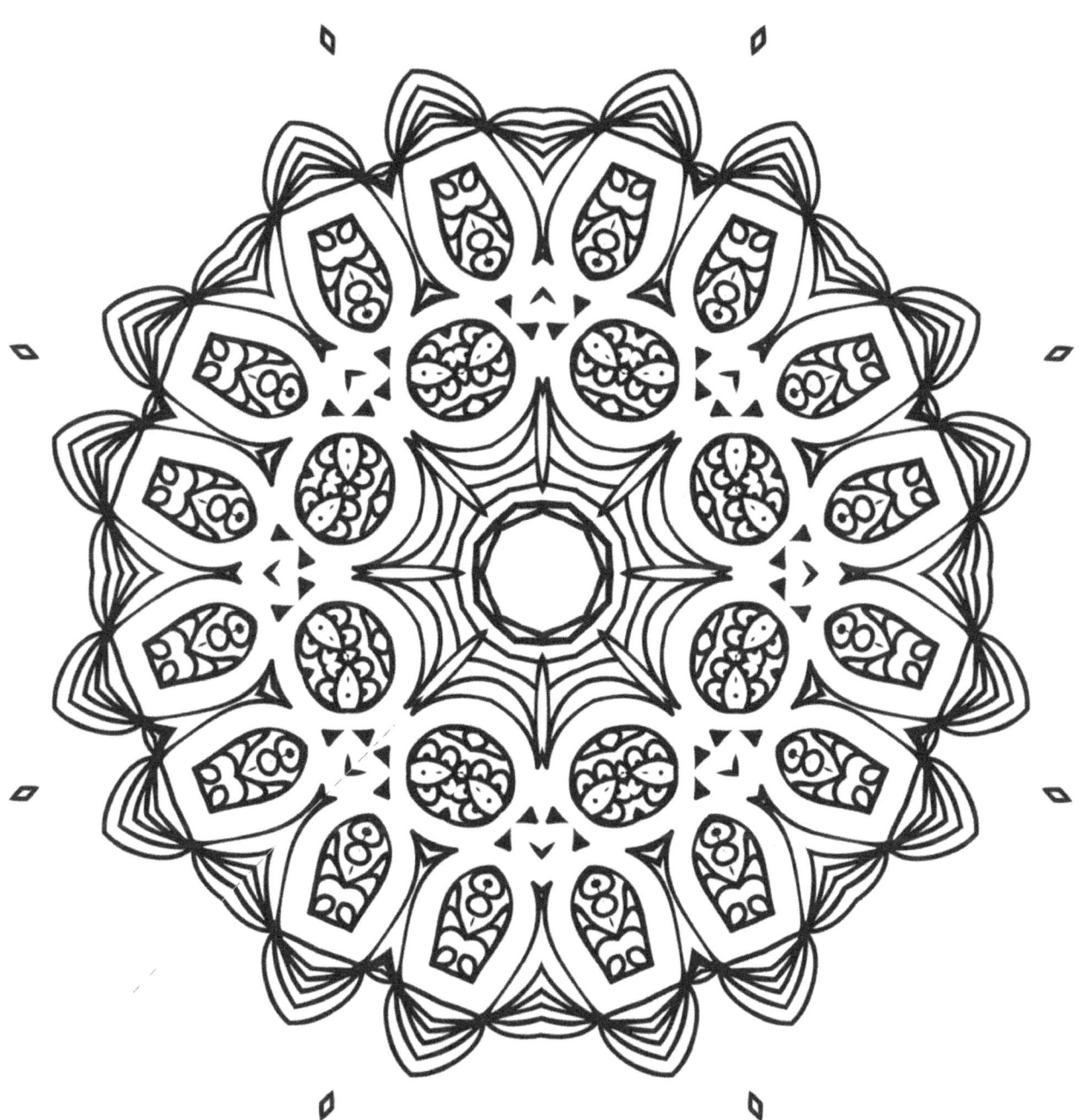

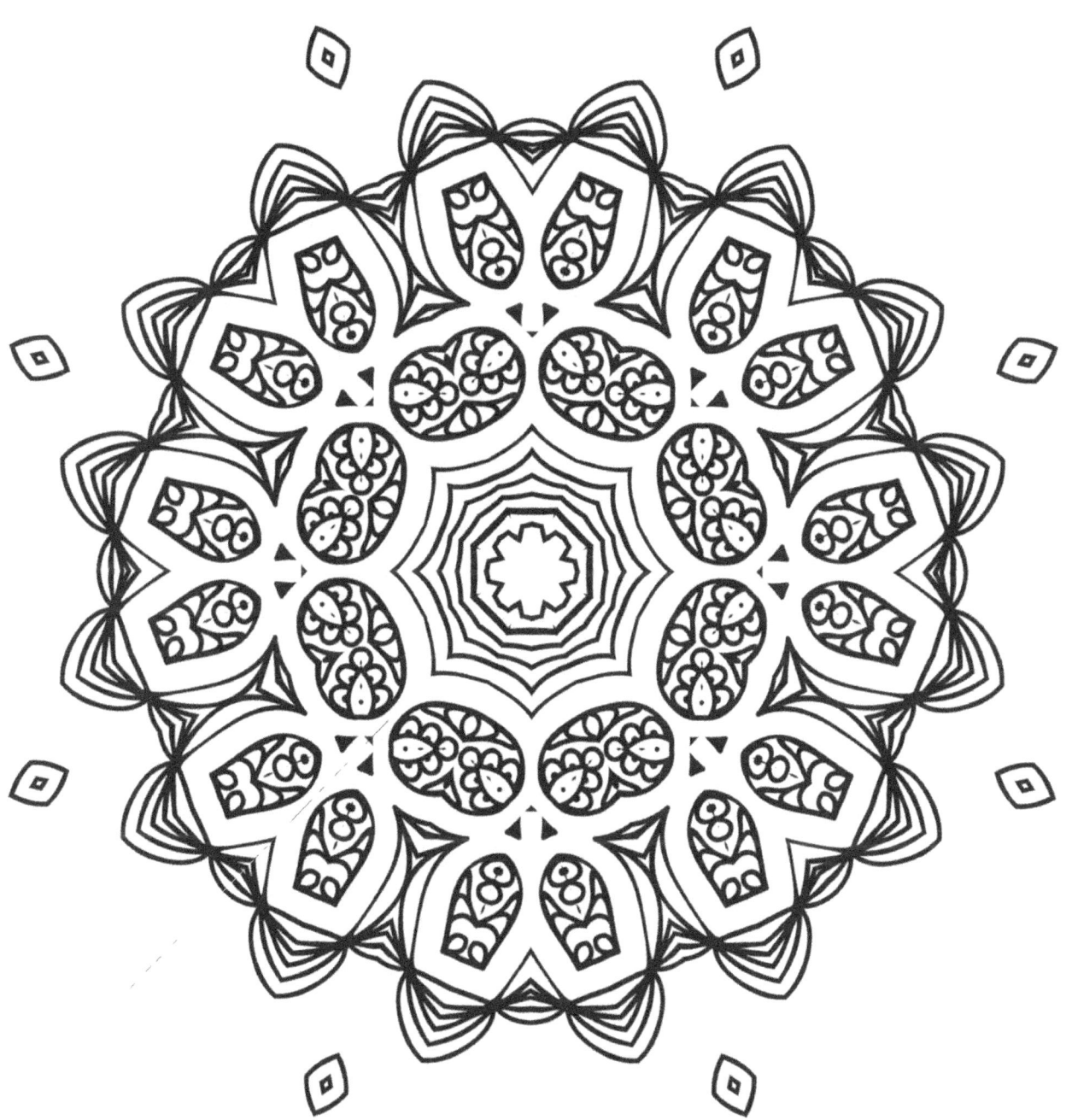

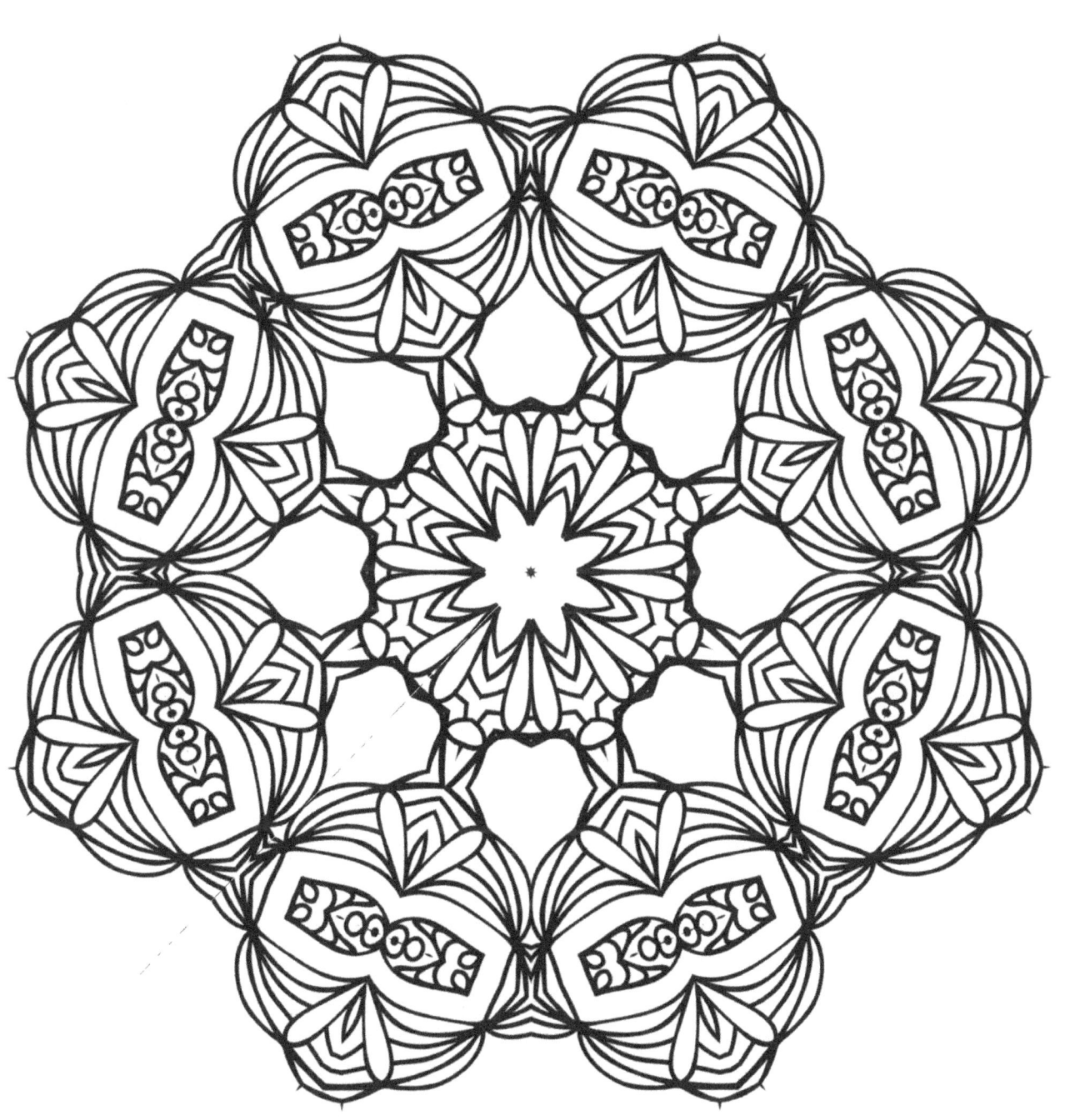

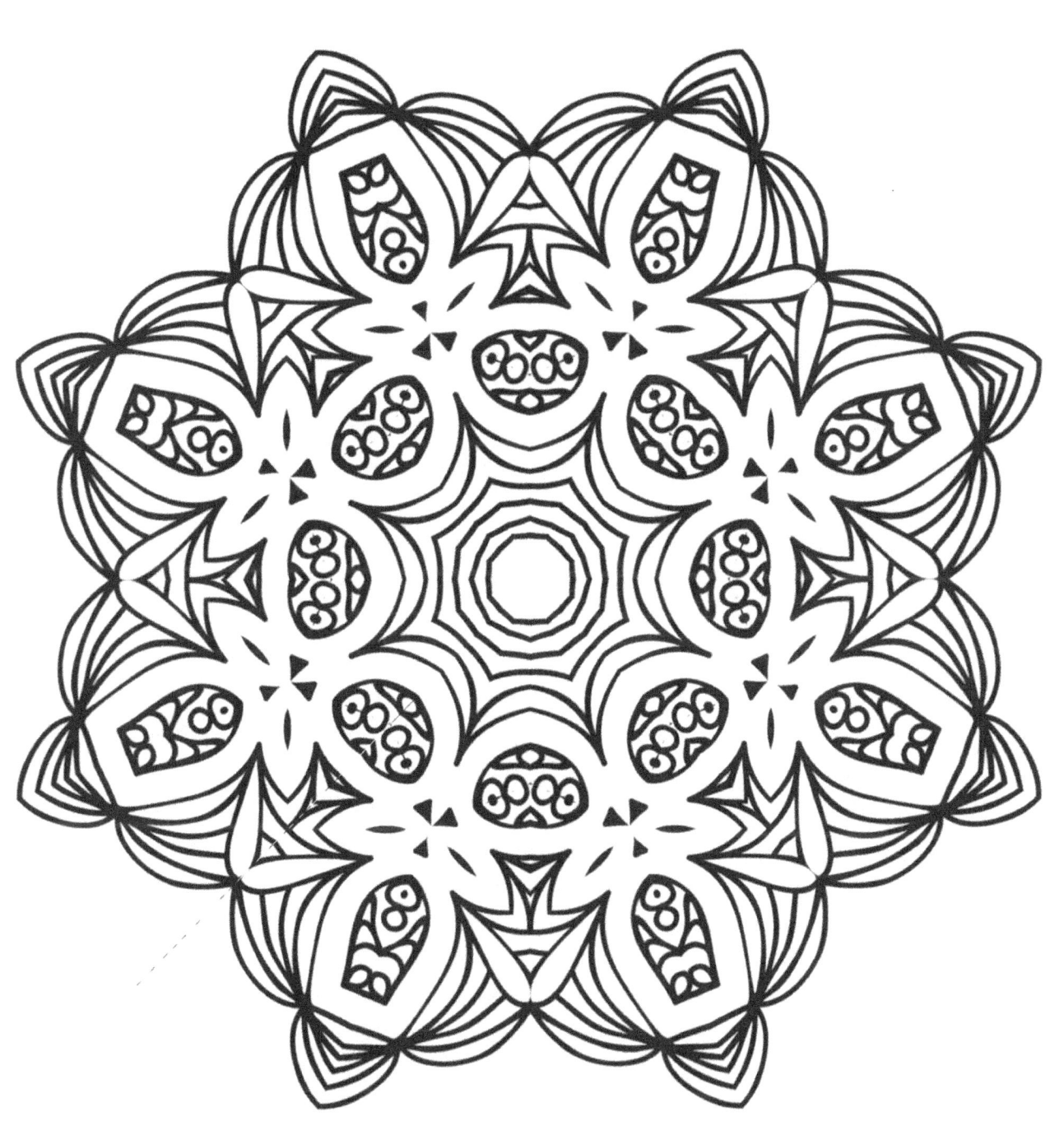

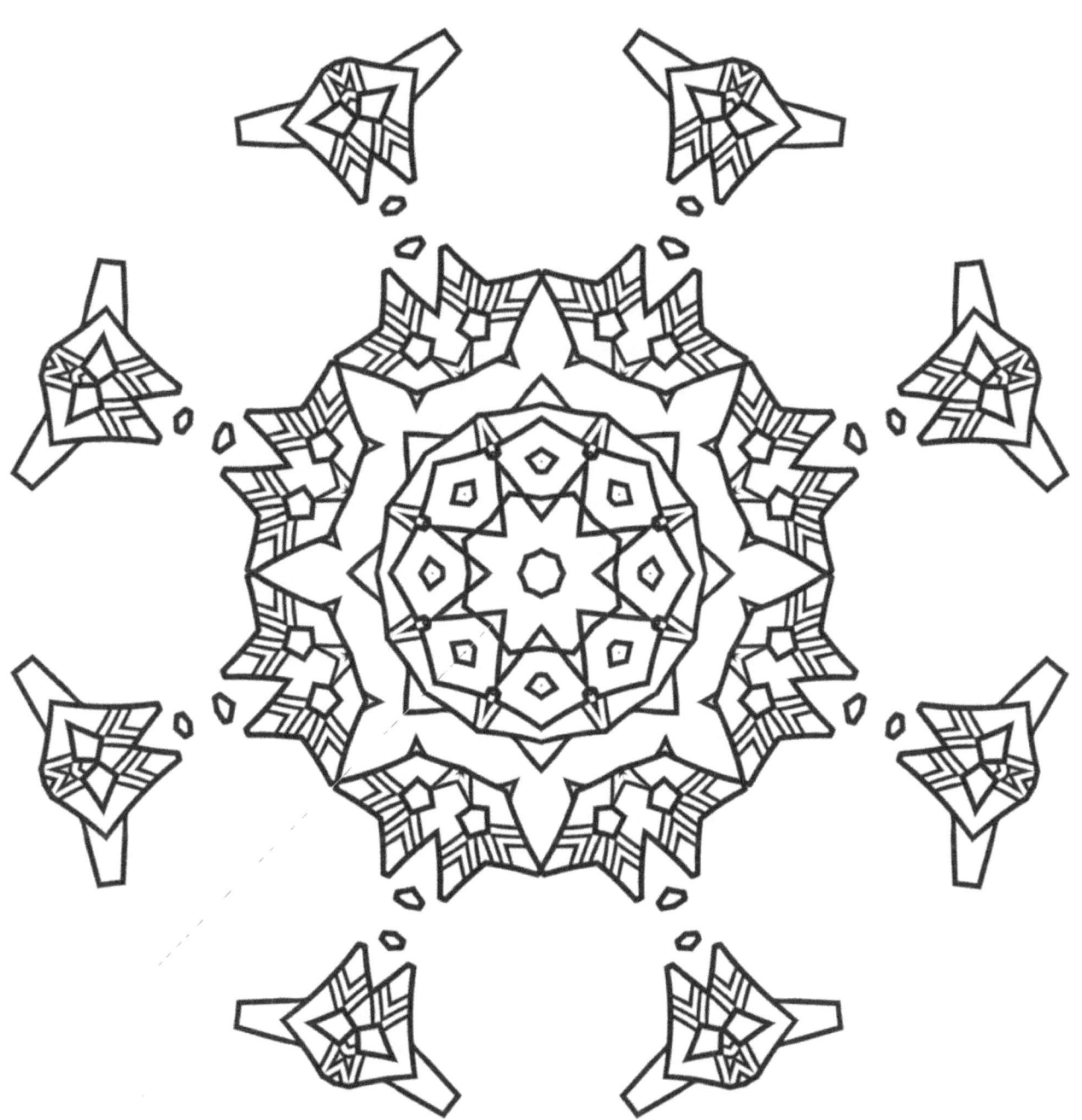

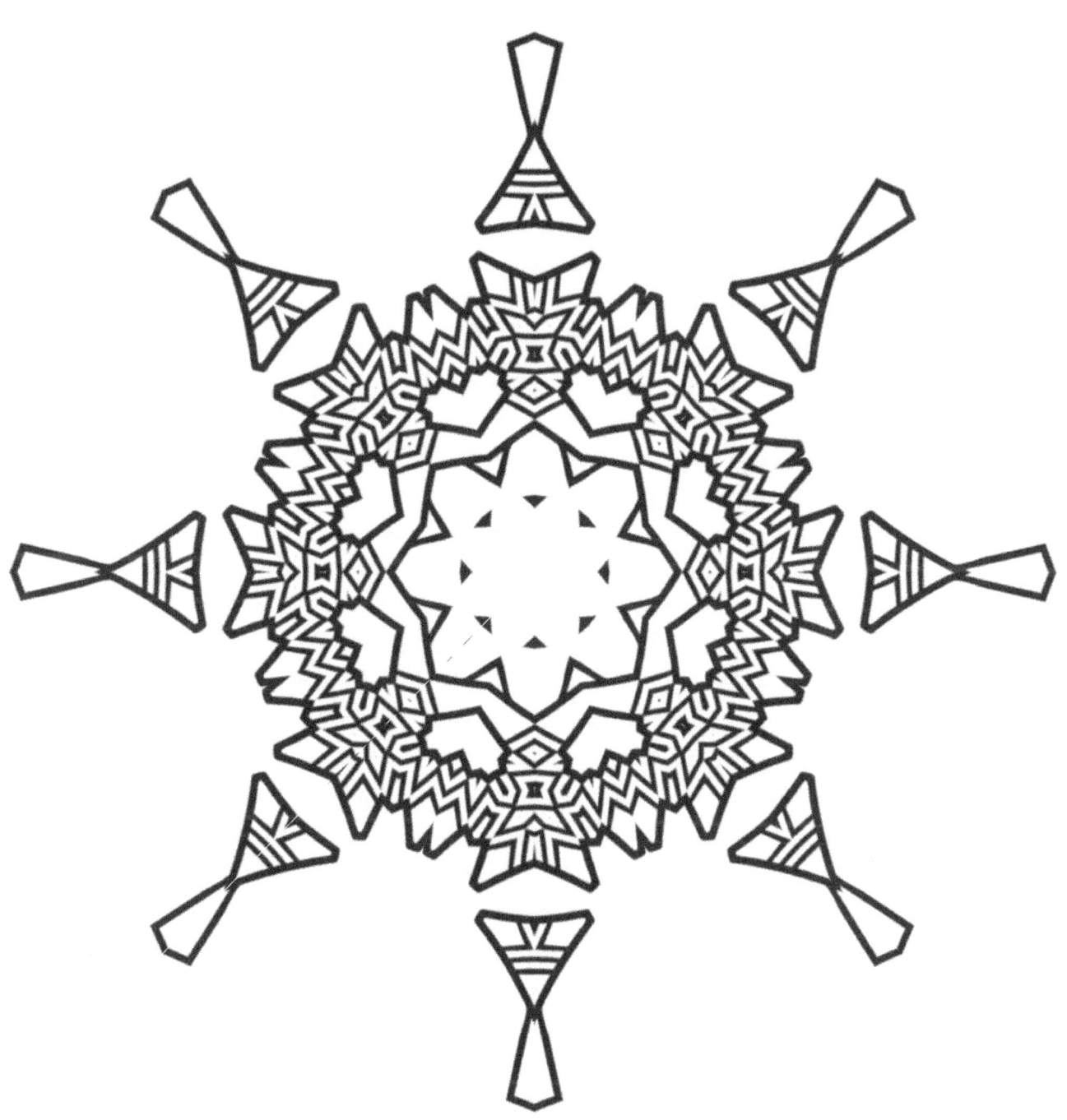

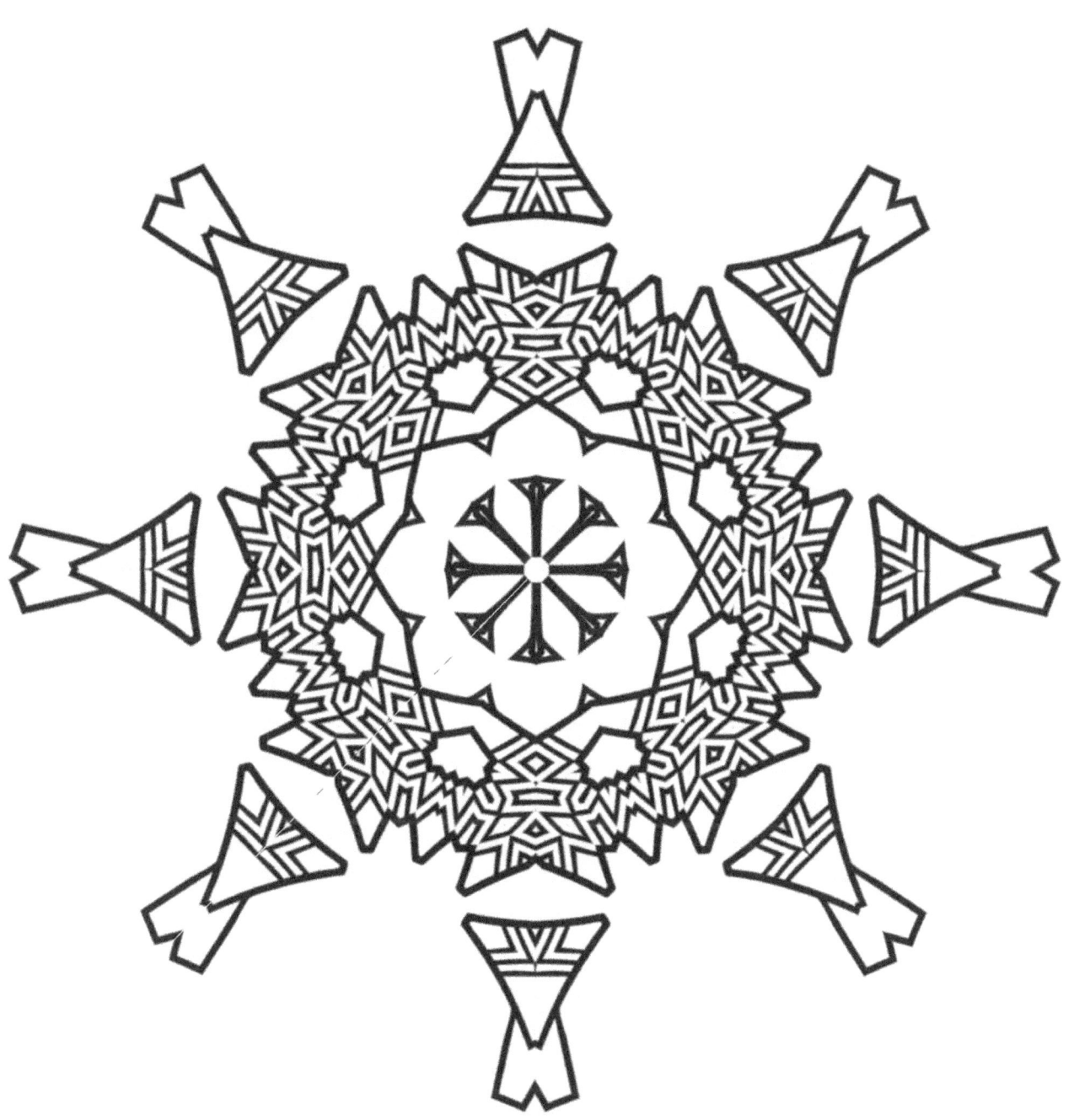

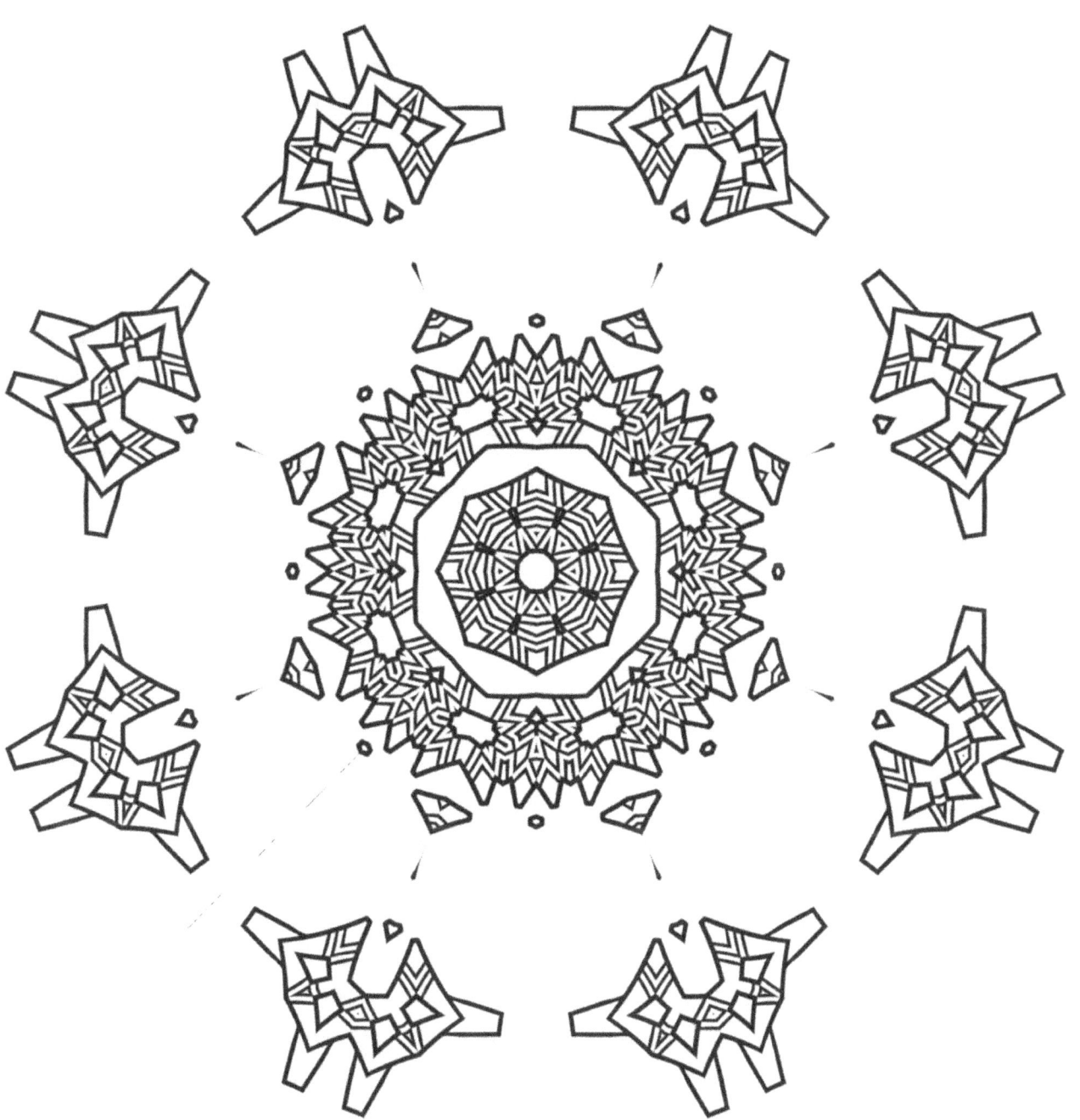

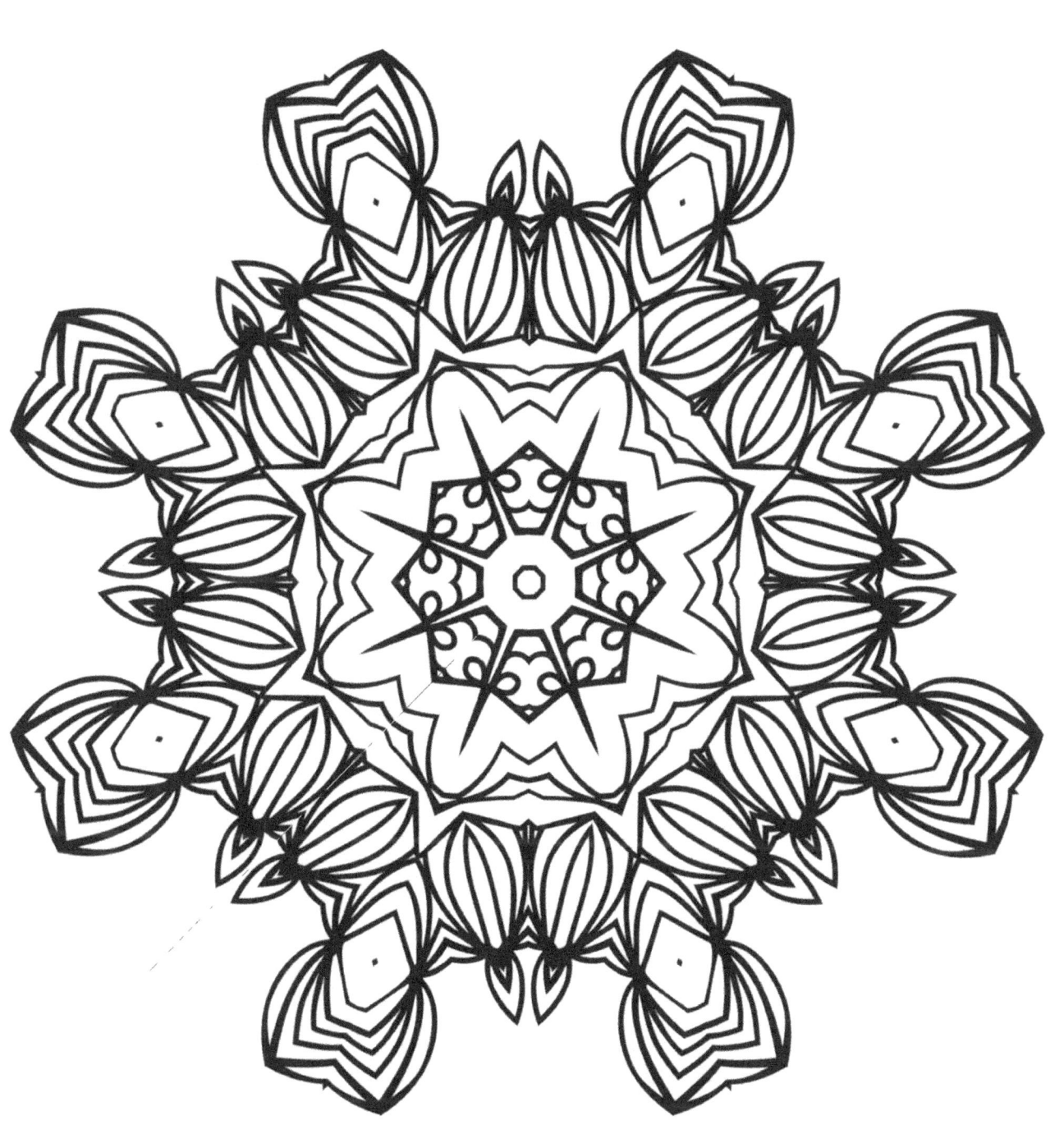

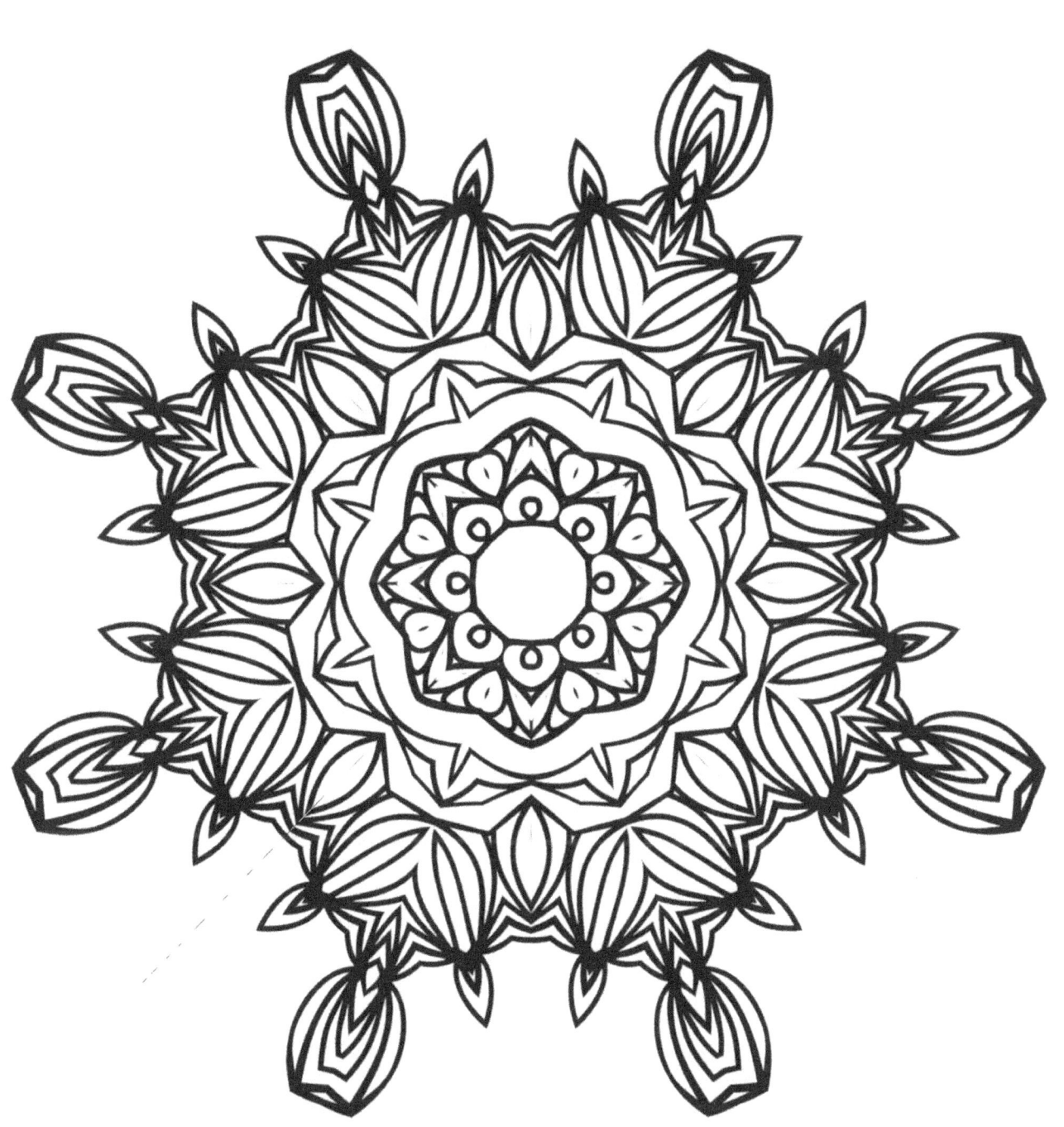

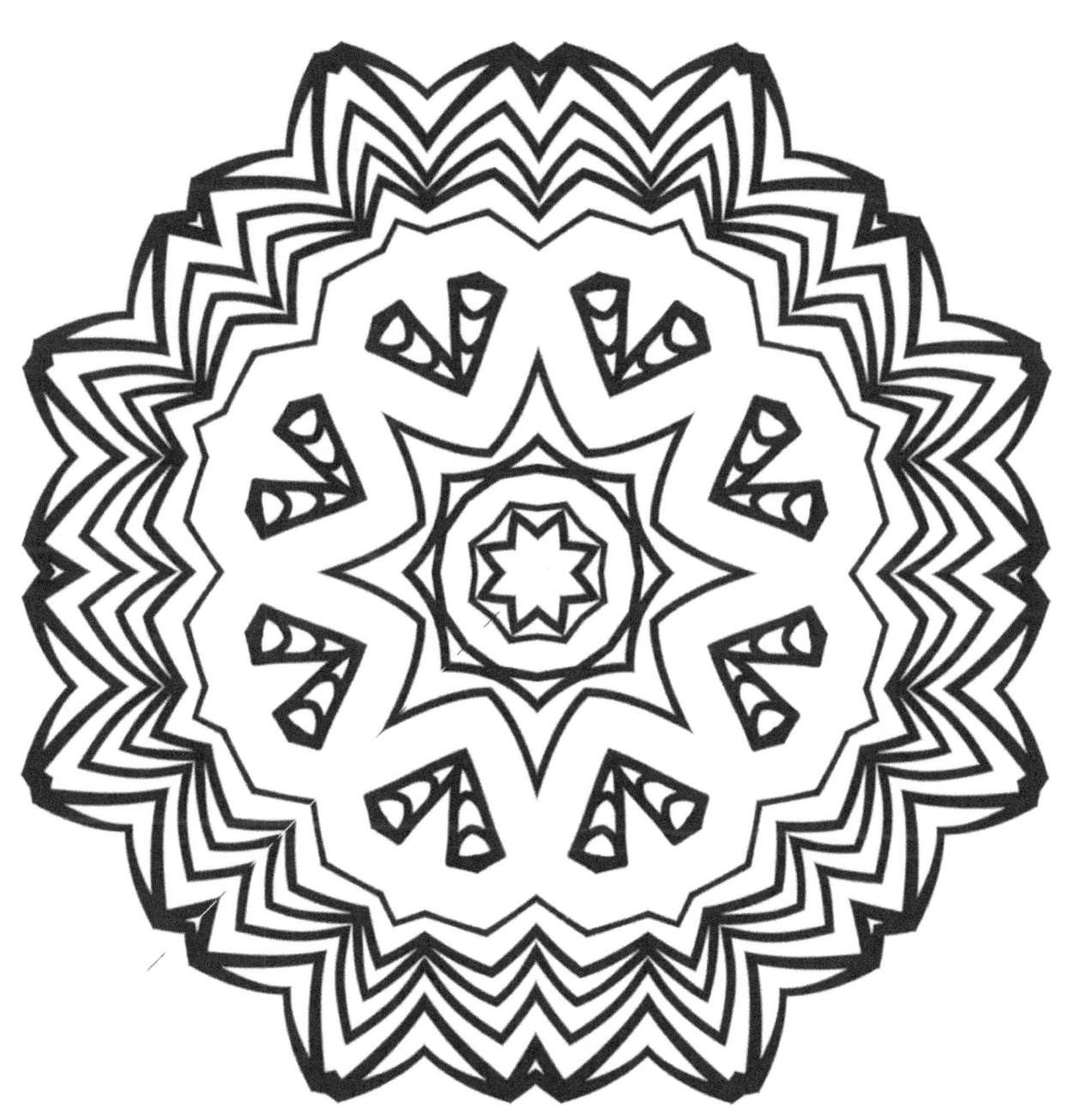

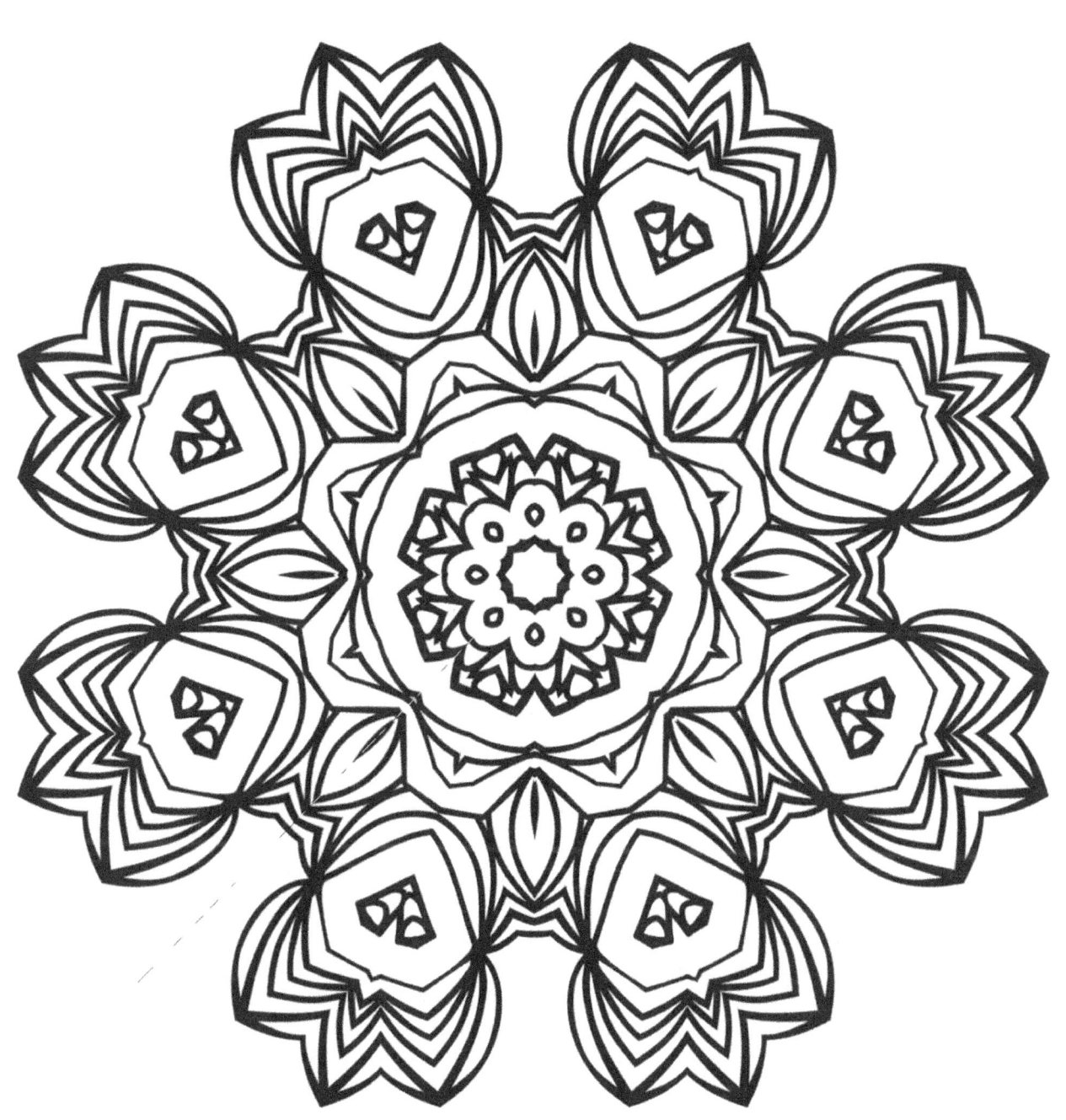

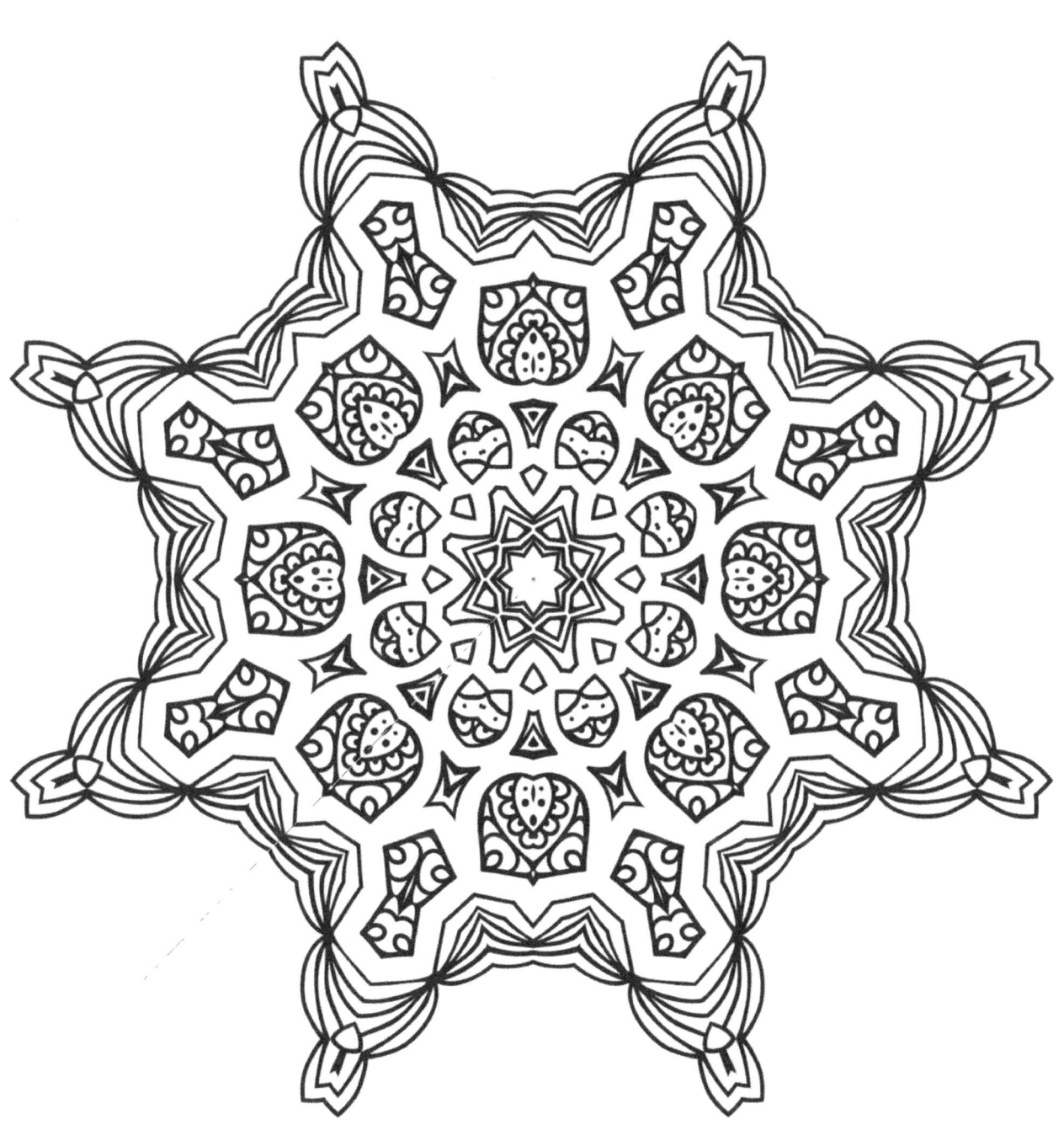

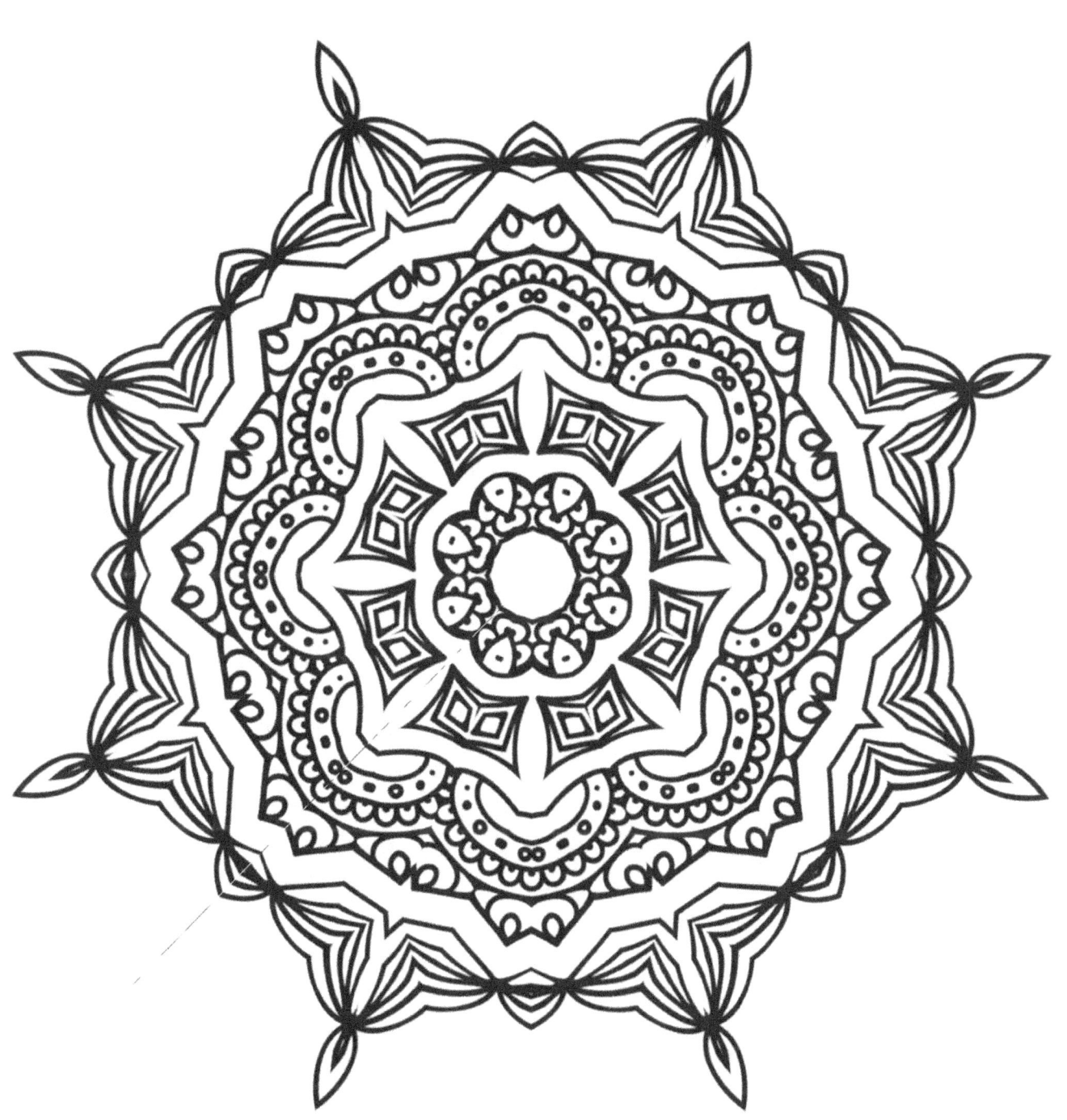

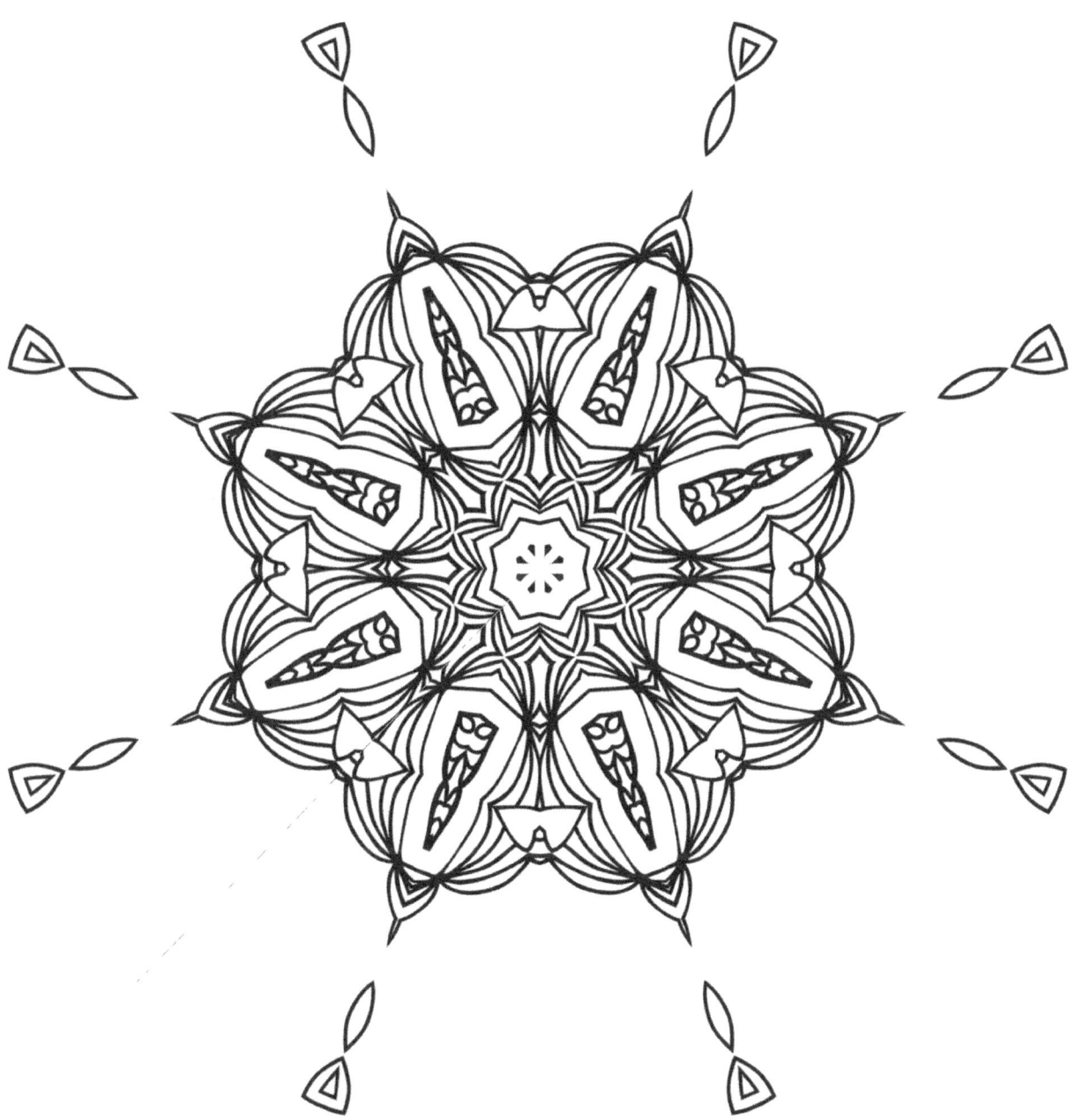

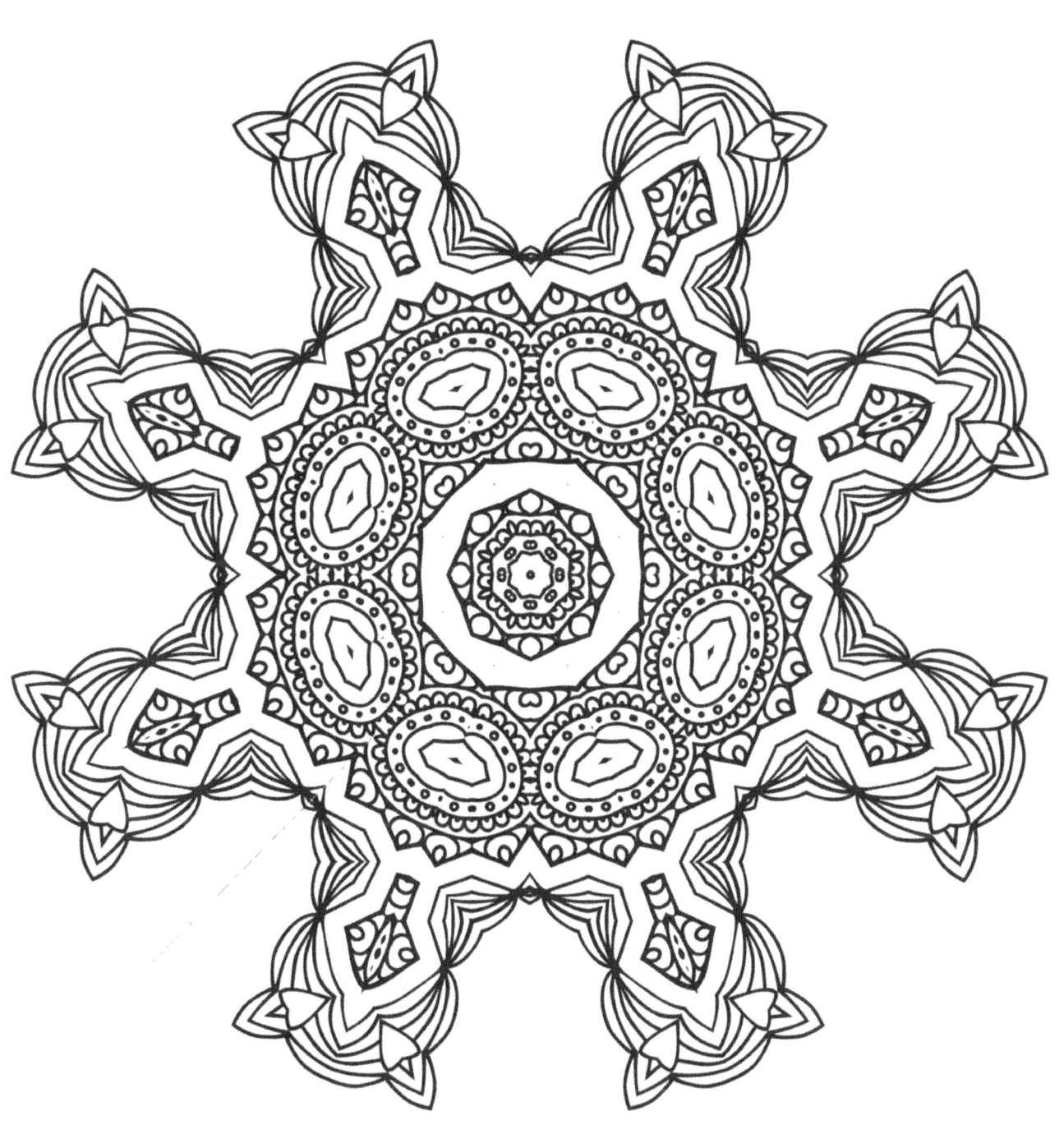

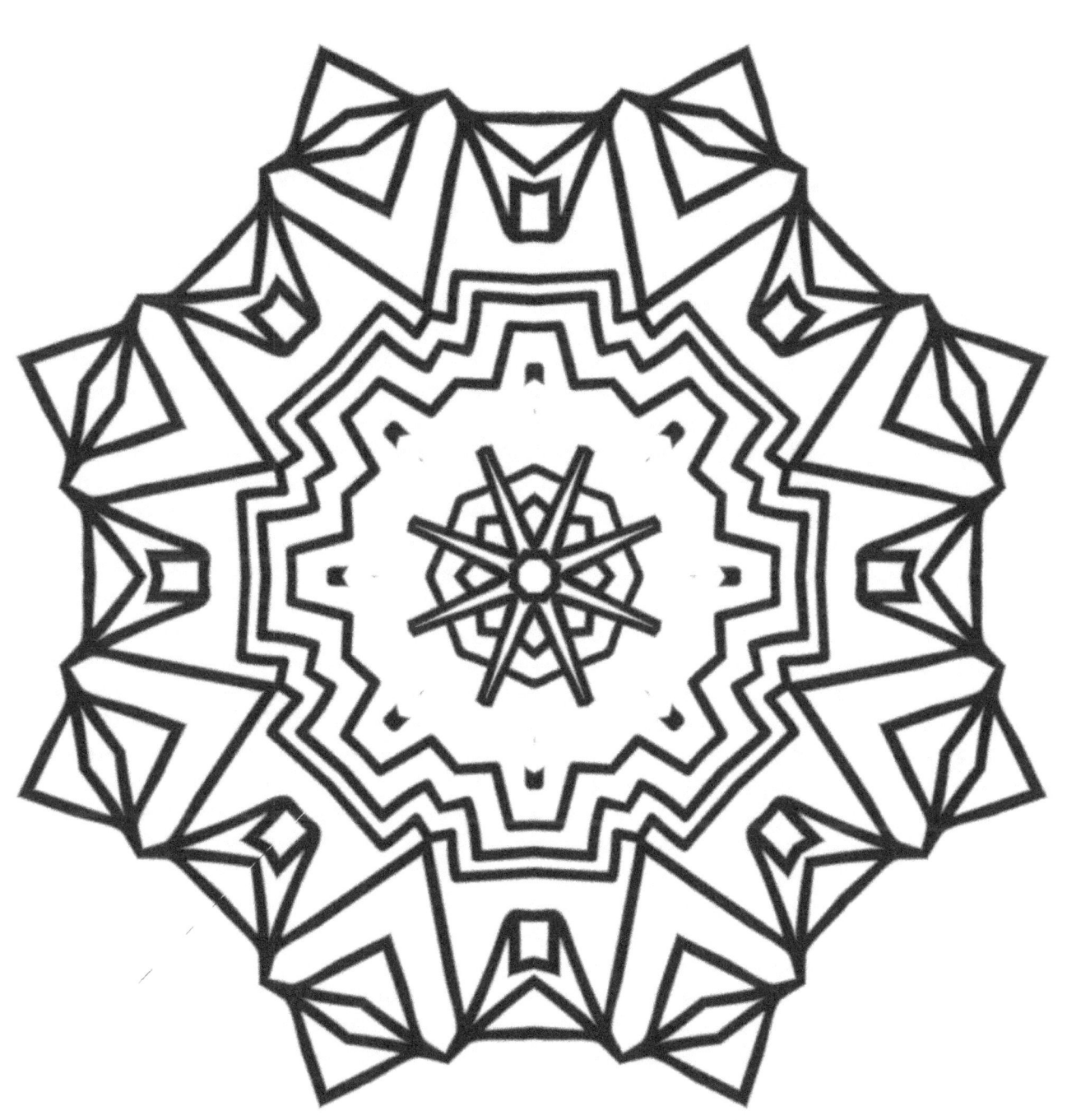

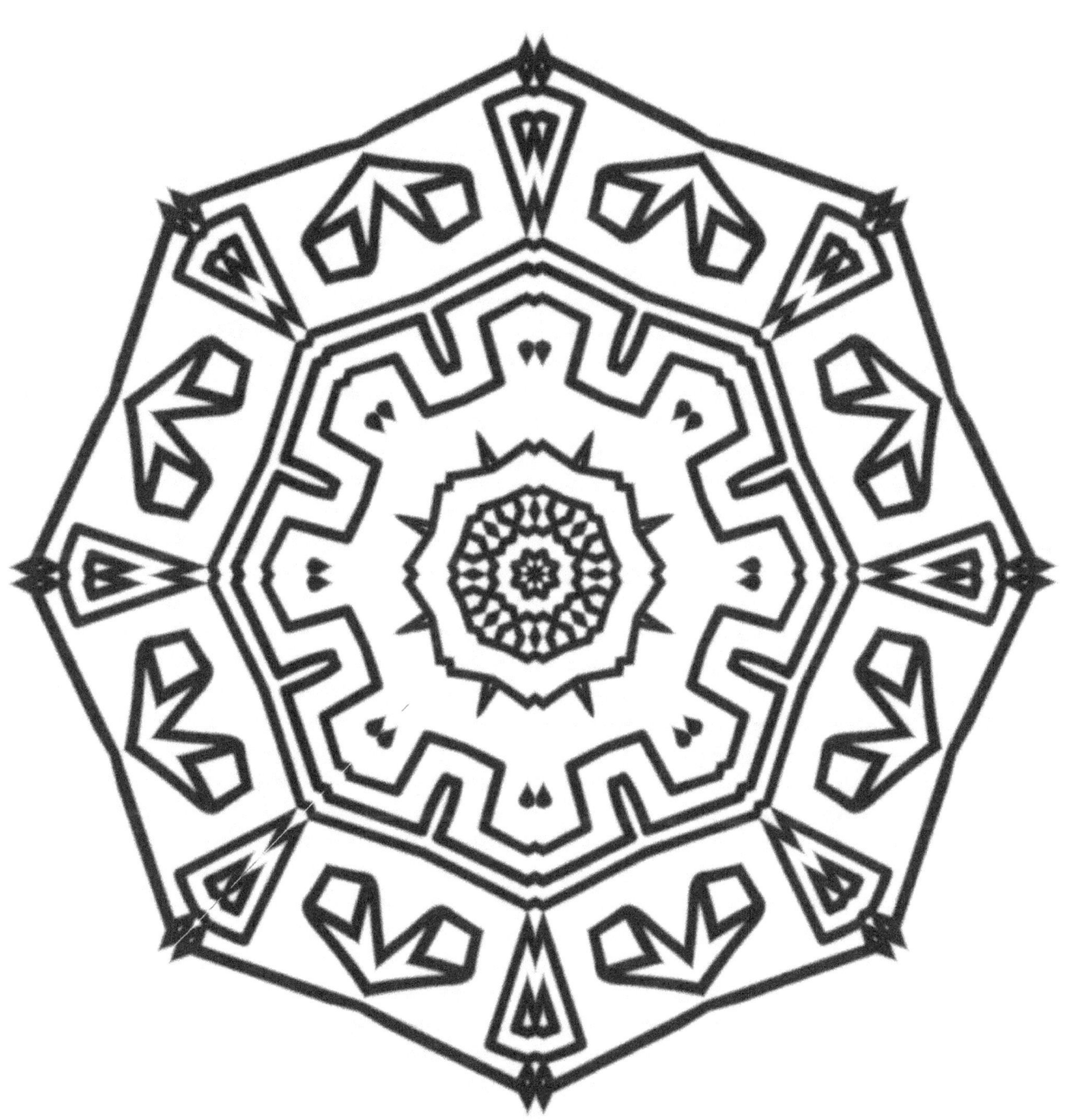

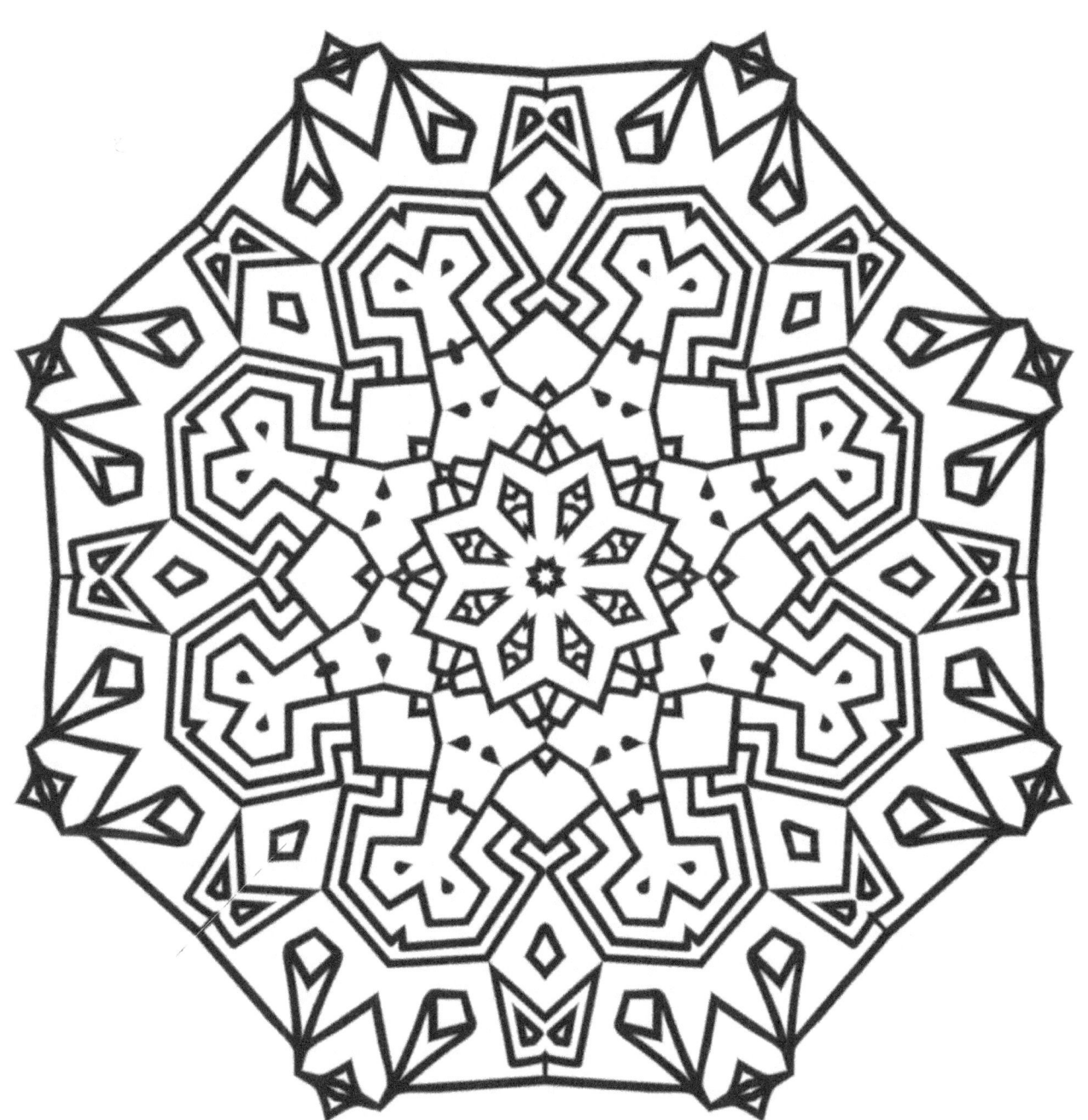

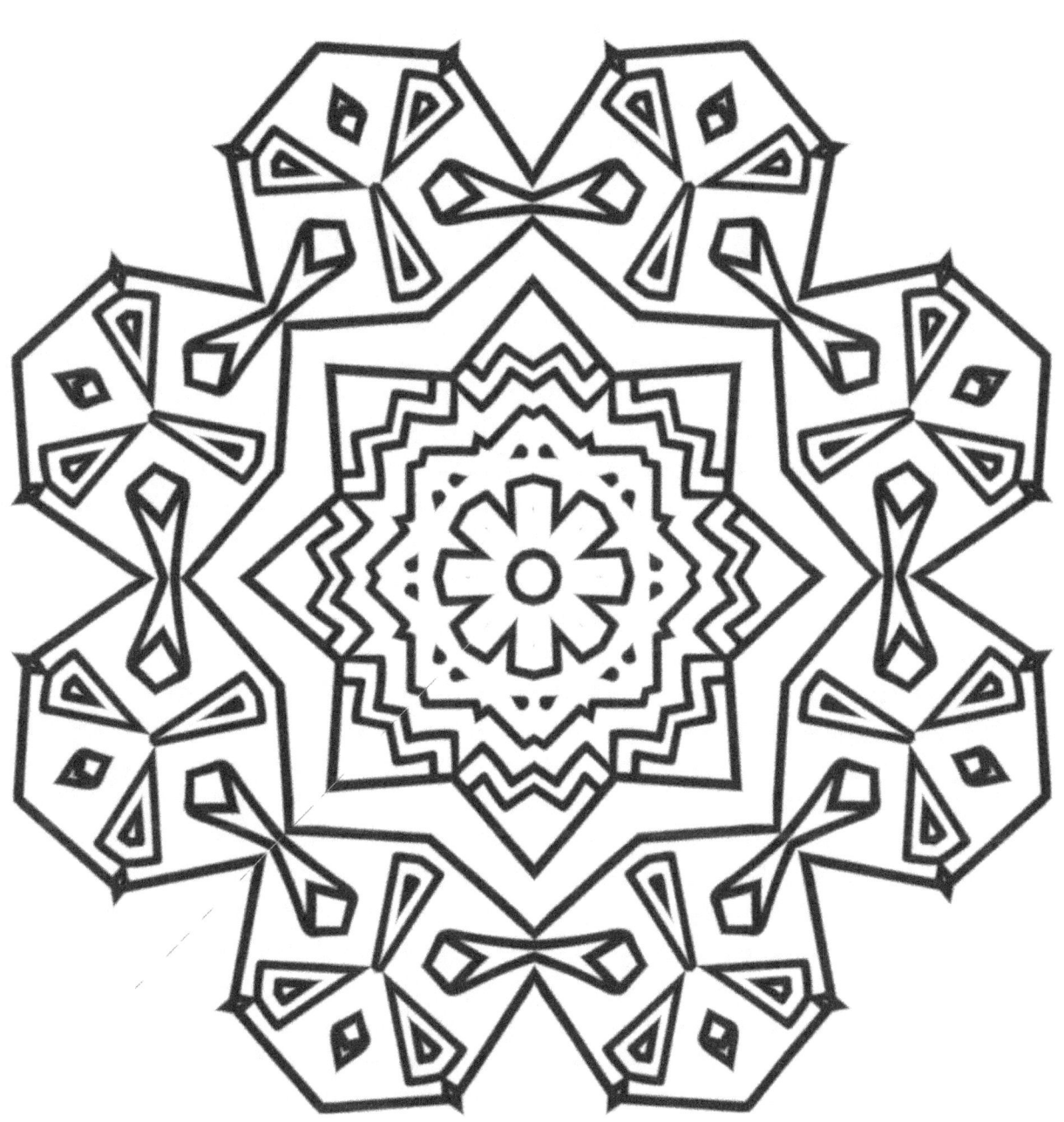

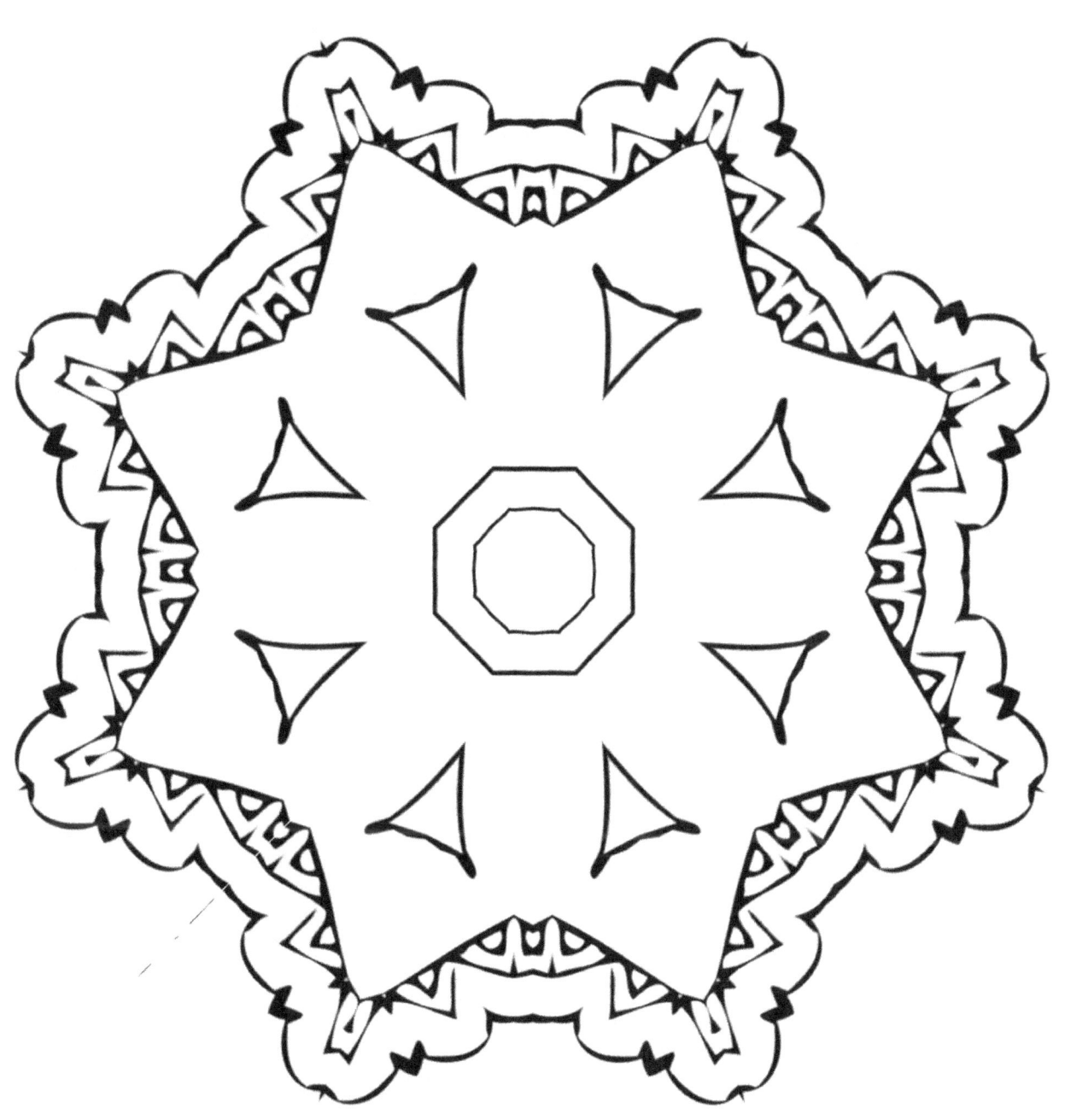

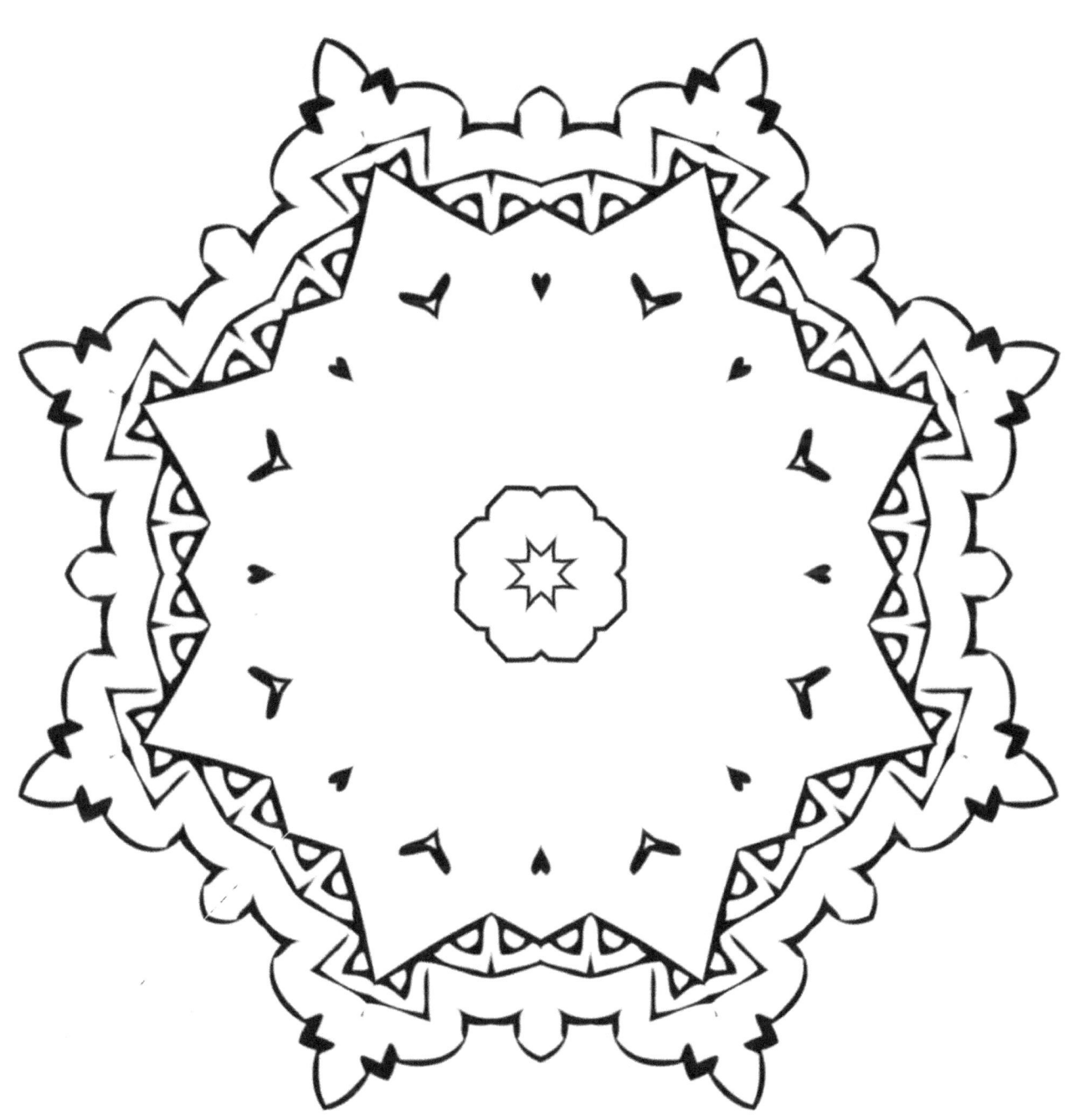

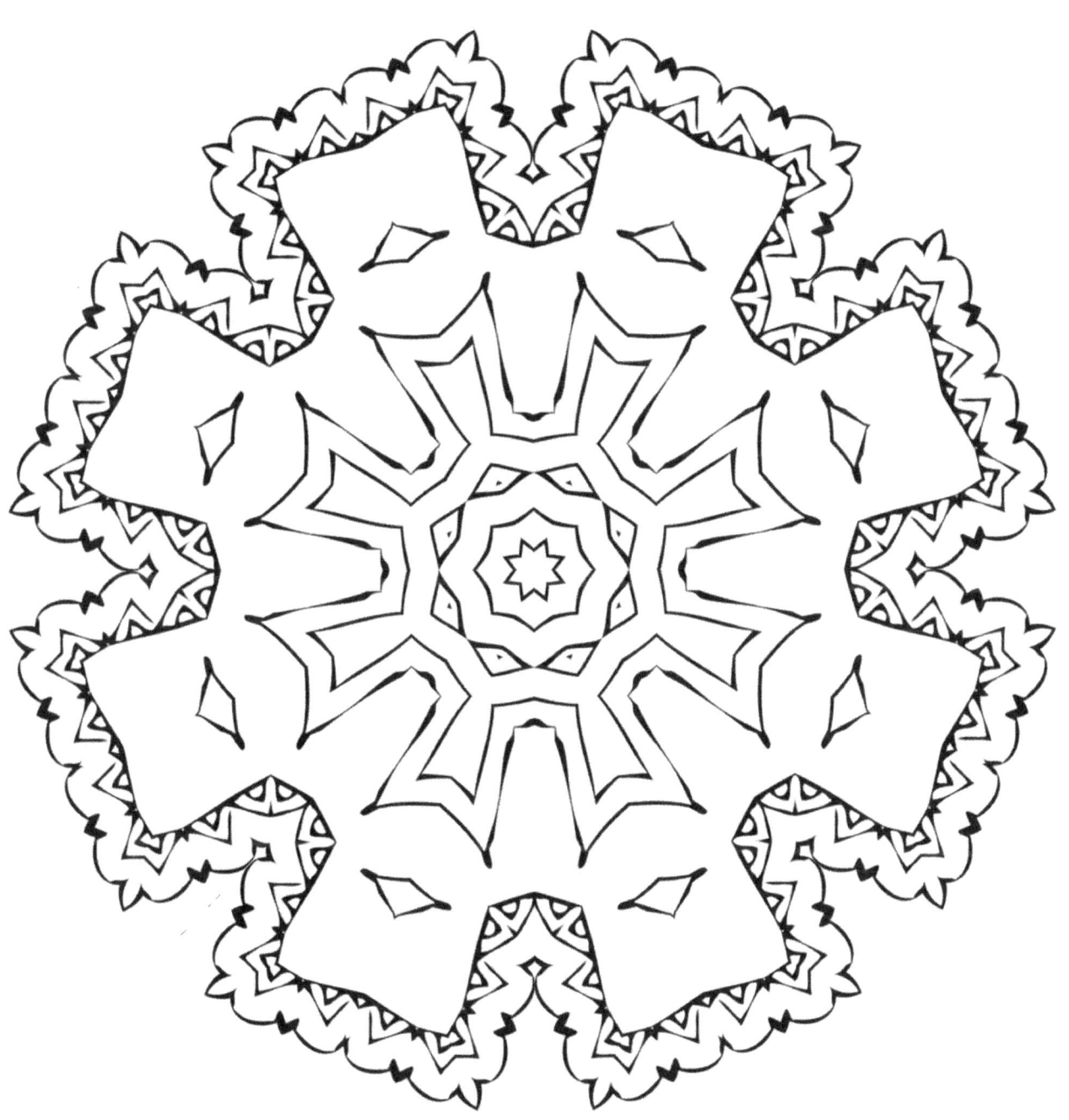

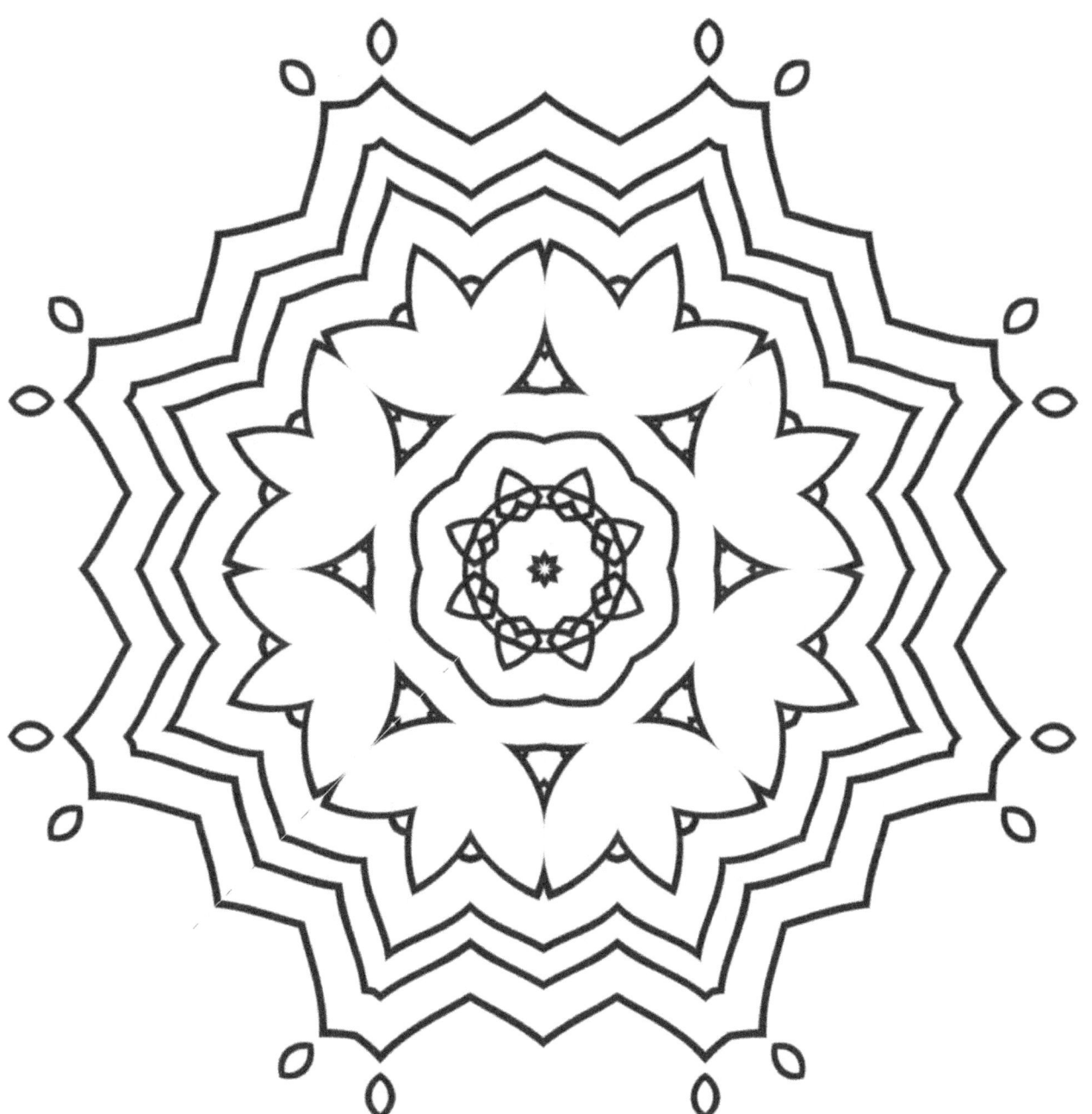

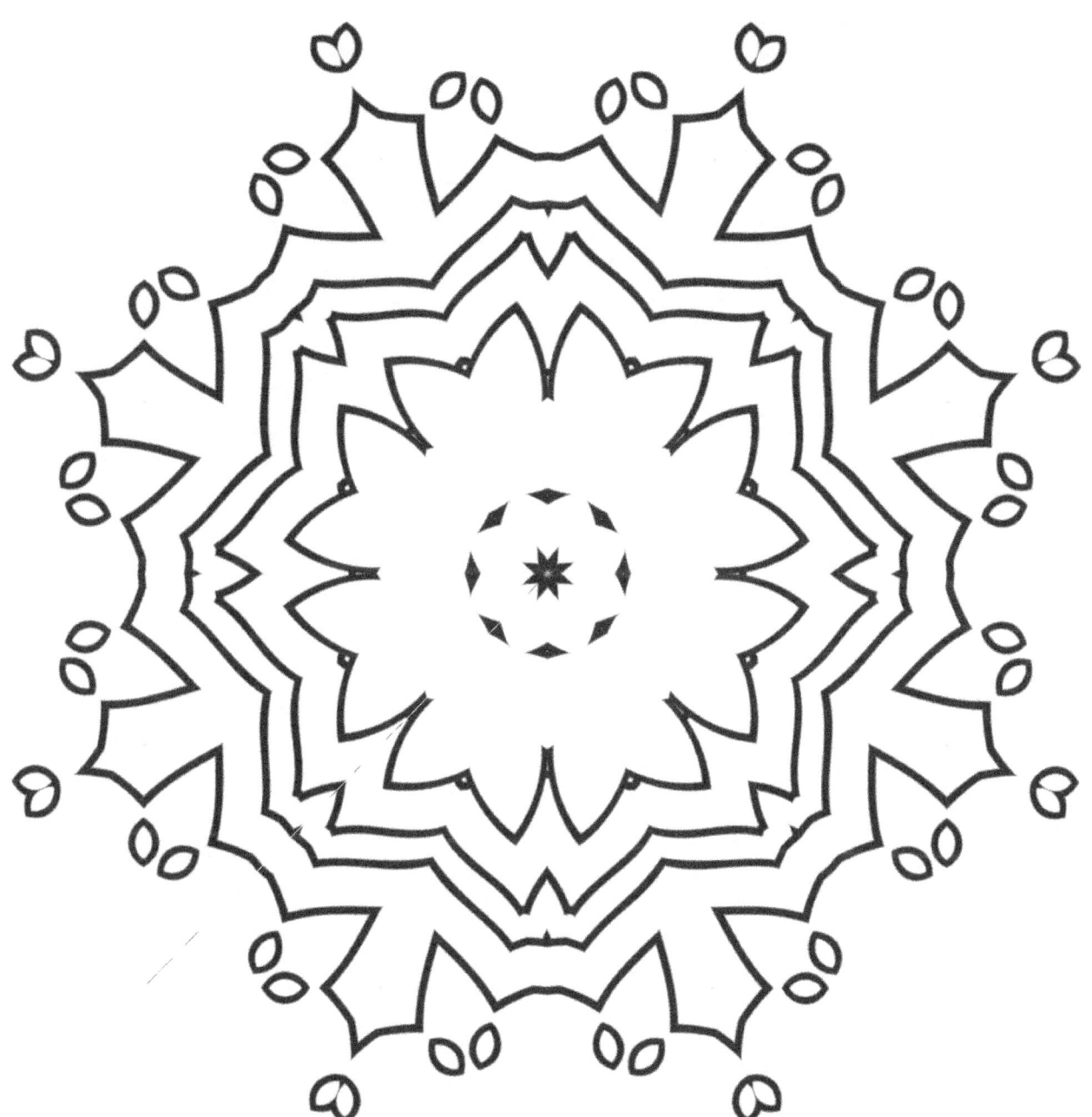

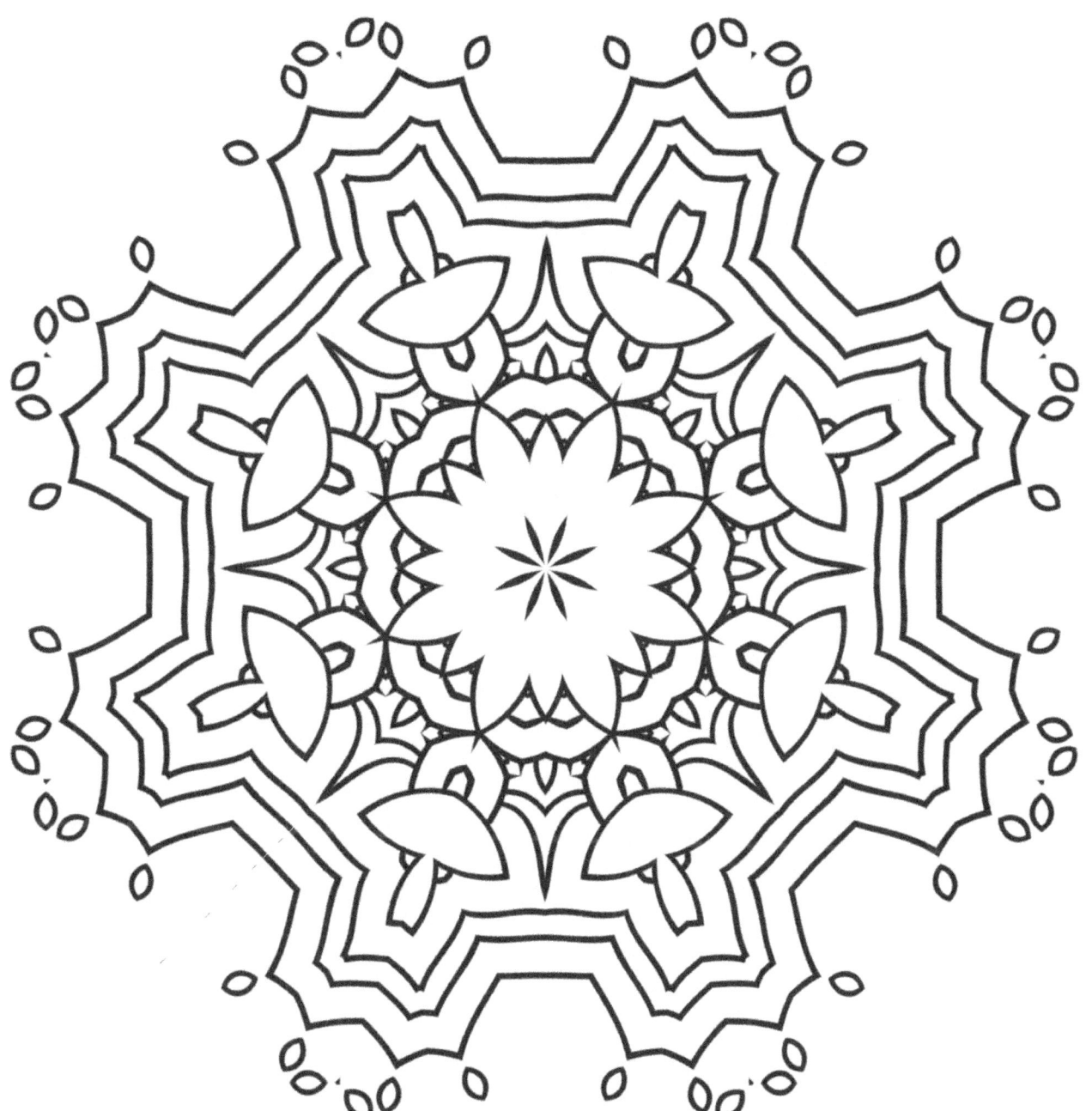

PDF Version of this book : http://bit.ly/easy_madalas2

Don't Miss Another our Books.

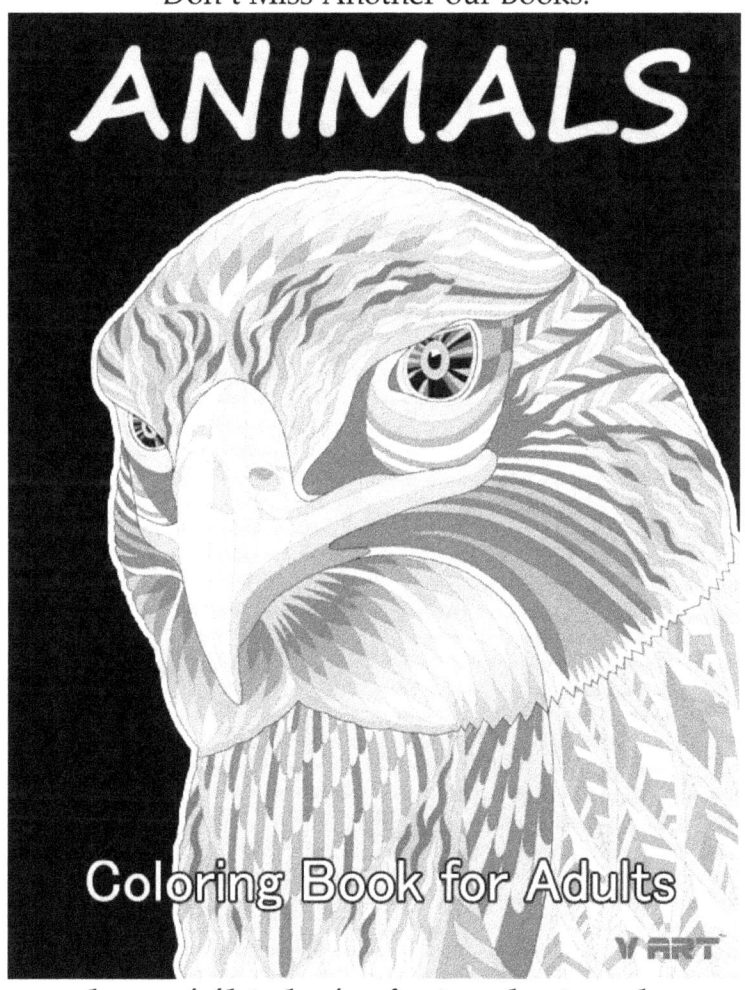

http://bit.ly/safari_coloring_b

ISBN : 9781523987931
(Use this ISBN for searching on amazon.com)

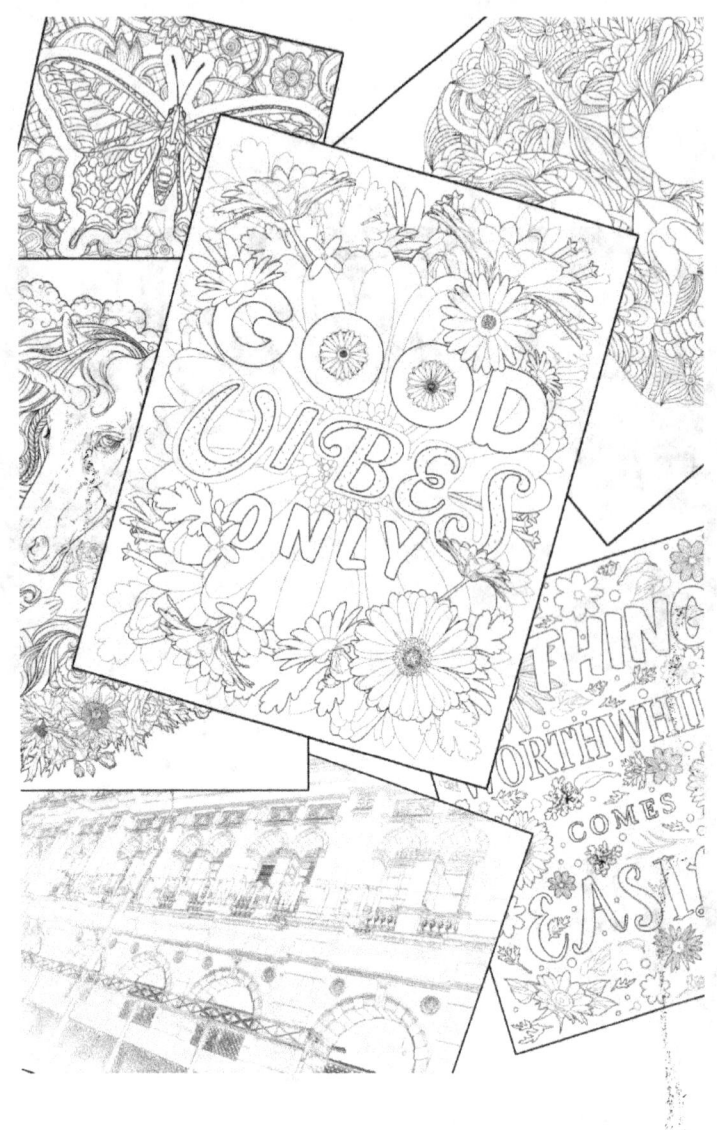

Join Us >> http://bit.ly/get_sample_free

- Get Free "Reviw Copies" of our New releases
- Exclusive offers and book giveaways
- More events from our community

Thank you

www.ingramcontent.com/pod-product-compliance
Lightning Source LLC
Chambersburg PA
CBHW081837170526
45167CB00007B/2835